The Mezquita and Medina Azahara: The Hist
Most Famous Landmarks in Cordoba, Spain

By Charles River Editors

Amjad Sheikh's picture of the Mosque-Cathedral of Córdoba

About Charles River Editors

Charles River Editors provides superior editing and original writing services across the digital publishing industry, with the expertise to create digital content for publishers across a vast range of subject matter. In addition to providing original digital content for third party publishers, we also republish civilization's greatest literary works, bringing them to new generations of readers via ebooks.

Sign up here to receive updates about free books as we publish them, and visit Our Kindle Author Page to browse today's free promotions and our most recently published Kindle titles.

Introduction

The Mezquita of Córdoba

Toni Castillo Quero's picture of the Mosque-Cathedral of Córdoba

"To Córdoba belong all the beauty and ornaments that delight the eye or dazzle the sight. Her long line of Sultans form her crown of glory; her necklace is strung with the pearls which her poets have gathered from the ocean of language; her dress is of the banners of learning, well-knit together by her men of science; and the masters of every art and industry are the hem of her garments..." – Stanley Lane-Poole, "The Moors in Spain"

The Calle Cardenal Herrero in Córdoba is an iconic cobbled street impossible to overlook, for it is home to the Andalusian city's spectacular Mosque-Cathedral. Also known as "La Mezquita," this one-of-a-kind Moorish and Christian place of worship reels in about 1.5 million visitors each year, most of whom find themselves spellbound by its hypnotic architectural features and the riveting history that has transpired and continues to within the beautifully weathered walls of the dual-church. That said, the Mezquita is far more than a mere tourist attraction - in recent years, the Mosque-Cathedral of Córdoba has become the crux of a complicated religious conflict resurrected by impassioned worshipers and patriotic locals who fear not only for the future of its legacy, but the preservation of its true history.

It is easy for those on the outside looking in to make hasty judgments about the ongoing dispute, considering the endless amount of information that is uploaded online by the second. The contentious debates surrounding the Mezquita are often products of outdated prejudices, festering distrust, and whitewashing, all of which make it harder for the Mezquita to remain a non-discriminatory space serviceable to and appreciated by everyone today.

The Medina Azahara

A picture of the reception hall

"To Córdoba belong all the beauty and ornaments that delight the eye or dazzle the sight. Her long line of Sultans form her crown of glory; her necklace is strung with the pearls which her poets have gathered from the ocean of language; her dress is of the banners of learning, well-knit together by her men of science; and the masters of every art and industry are the hem of her garments..." – Stanley Lane-Poole, "The Moors in Spain"

Love, as they often say, is best expressed through meaningful actions, as opposed to syrupy words and hollow promises. To pragmatists, it's the smaller things that make the biggest splash, while hopeless romantics may take it upon themselves to go the extra mile. Apart from showering their better halves with trips abroad to bucket-list destinations and mountains of extravagant gifts, the wealthy might organize benefits and galas, and make handsome donations to a cause that deeply resonates with their loved one.

Whereas most would deem the tokens of affection exchanged by celebrity power couples to be sweet, but inordinately excessive, many of those who pine after storybook romances are especially enamored of these grand gestures. However, nobody can deny that they've produced some of the most famous works in the world, including buildings such as the Taj Mahal.

Such stories can certainly send the hearts of the starry-eyed aflutter, and while love is not quantifiable, few love stories can compare to the blissful fairy-tale attached to the Madinat al-Zahra, commonly known today as the Medina Azahara. This tale involved a king named Abd ar-Rahman who was so besotted with a maiden that he built an entire palace-city for her from scratch. Naturally, this wasn't just any old city – covering well over a million square meters by the foothills of the Cordoban Sierra Morena Mountains, this was allegedly the largest palace-city ever built in Europe.

The Mezquita and Medina Azahara: The History and Legacy of the Moors' Most Famous Landmarks in Córdoba, Spain offers a virtual tour of this priceless place of worship, and how it has been at the center of religious debates for hundreds of years. Along with pictures of important people, places, and events, you will learn about the Mezquita and Medina Azahara like never before.

The Mezquita and Medina Azahara: The History and Legacy of the Moors' Most Famous Landmarks in Córdoba, Spain

About Charles River Editors

Introduction

   An Ancient House of Worship

   The Aljama

   A Love Story for the Ages

   A Palace-City to Rival the Kingdom of God

   An Unexcelled Show of Prestige

   All that Glitters is Not Gold

   The Final Moorish Expansions

   The Return of the Christians

   Identity Crisis

   Online Resources

   Bibliography

Free Books by Charles River Editors

Discounted Books by Charles River Editors

An Ancient House of Worship

"For nearly eight centuries, under the Mohamedan rule, Spain set all Europe a shining example of a civilized and enlightened state. Her fertile provinces rendered doubly prolific, by the industrious engineering skill of the conquerors bore fruit a hundredfold, cities innumerable sprang up in the rich valleys in the Guadalquivir and the Guadiana whose names, and names only commemorate the vanished glories of their past." – Stanley Lane-Poole, "The Moors in Spain"

The sacred ground upon which the "Soul of Córdoba" stands seemed destined from the beginning of time to house a majestic worshiping place. Well over 2,000 years ago, and approximately 989 years before the conception of the present Mezquita, this plot of land hosted a worshiping ground for the Romans who invaded Córdoba, or as it was known then, "Córduba." The ancient Romans first came upon and conquered the lush and fruitful region of Córduba in the year 206 BCE, courtesy of Lucio Mario. This abrupt transition in power, dictated by the conclusion of what is now remembered as the "Battle of Ilipa," saw the Romans lay claim to virtually all of the Guadalquivir River Valley. Lucio Mario, who had spearheaded the successful campaign that drove out the Iberians at Alcala del Rio (close to what is now Seville), proceeded to erect the first Roman establishment there, a town they christened "Itálica."

For the next seven centuries, the Romans reigned over the region, and by 152 BCE, Itálica, now under General Claudio Marcelo's rule, had become recognized as a "colonia" and was the capital of the Roman province known as the "Hispania Ulterior." The city settlement had transformed into the Romans' chief military base during their war against the Lucitanian leader, Viriathus, and two of the milestones – a pair of stone pillars that served as signposts – that once marked the ancient cities of Carmo, Seville, and Tarraco via the Via Augusta now flank the main entrance of the Mosque-Cathedral.

As Itálica continued to flourish, the Romans continued to build settlements throughout the terrain, including one founded at the Andalusian port of Córduba, by the furthermost limits of the Guadalquivir River. The port bustled with activity, enlivened by merchants hawking their products and large vessels brimming with olive oil, wine, and other exports en route to Rome.

As a token of gratitude to the gods who had aided their victory over the Iberians and continued to watch over their thriving Spanish settlements, the Romans produced various temples to a number of deities. One of the grandest temples, devoted to the god Janus, was built opposite the still-standing Roman Bridge of Córdoba on the Guadalquivir. Some have asserted this temple stood right where the Mosque-Cathedral now stands.

According to the Romans, Janus, the "god of beginnings," januae (doorways), and jani (archways), was the same deity who fathered Tiberinus with the nymph Camasene, and Tiberinus became the inspiration behind the name of the Tiber River. This powerful deity was depicted with either two or four faces, the latter of which symbolized "the spirit of the 4-way arch." To the Romans, his unique and literally multi-faceted appearance allowed him to see simultaneously what was in front and behind him.

Strategic points in Rome, as well as its fringes, were guarded by several freestanding ceremonial archways that soldiers and civilians passed through to enter and exit the city. The Janus Geminus, situated to the north of the Roman Forum, also doubled as a shrine for the god, and was as such among the most frequently used by Roman armies. This rectangular bronze block is punctured by "double-doors," or two arch-shaped openings on either side of it. Soldiers marched from one end of the structure to the other in ritualistic fashion before venturing out to battle, not only paying tribute, but requesting blessings of good fortune from Janus. Legend has it that the double-doors of the Roman jani were kept shut during times of peace and left open during times of war. Given the turbulence of the political atmosphere and the barbaric problem-solving tactics generally employed during this era, it was rarely the former case.

While Janus is most commonly affiliated with the guardianship of all entrances, travelers, and new beginnings, the 5th century historian Macrobius also characterized the deity as an intellectual and devout being who was once awarded honors for his piety. This is all the more noteworthy in light of the fact the spot became a Moorish intellectual center centuries later.

With the Janus temple long gone, modern historians can only imagine what the temple across the Guadalquivir looked like. Most likely, it was a smaller variant of the temple for Janus in the Roman Forum. This enclosure was probably created by two double-gates on either end, and featured a glinting bronze statue of Janus, each one of his scowling faces directed towards one gate. 1st century BCE chronicler Titus Livius reiterated the significance behind the temple in question, a shrine that acted "as an index of peace and war, that when open it might signify that the nation was in arms, when closed that all the peoples round about were pacified."

Under Claudio Marcelo, a new tradition began. Thenceforth, the Republic's consuls were to be sworn into office on the first day of January. Following the induction ceremony, the new consuls arrived at the temple to pay tribute to Janus, presenting to him heartfelt prayers and offerings of salted spelt, made from a type of wheat with "bearded ears" and "spikelets," and ianual, or barley cakes. Figs, dates, honey, wine, and incense were also gifted to the god in the hopes of acquiring a sweet year in return, filled with good harvests and prosperity. As such, this temple in Córduba would have been well-visited by officials and members of the public alike.

Regular sacrifices may have also been performed in the temple. Priests, recognized and otherwise, were assisted by slaves, who were tasked with the ritualistic grunt work. Sacrifices typically commenced at the crack of dawn, but dark, unlicensed ceremonies usually occurred in the dead of the night. The most superstitious celebrants supposedly offered to Janus non-castrated male victims, but such accounts are most likely exaggerated. Most priests offered slain, fully-grown animals such as lambs and cattle, accompanied by baskets of leavened bread, polenta, alica (boiled grain), sesame seeds, scaly fish, and jugs of oil.

With all of that said, some historians still question the existence of the Janus temple in Córduba altogether. A number of ancient sources made mention of this Janus-devoted temple in Córduba, but some historians in recent years, such as Professor Robert C. Knapp from the University of California, Berkeley, insist it never existed. Knapp believed historians from previous generations simply misread the milestones, which led to the understandable, but incorrect conclusion there was a Roman temple by the Guadalquivir.

By the 5th century CE, Córduba had yet another pivotal transformation. The Romans had finally met their match, vigorously resisting, but ultimately unable to fend off the band of Visigoths in their territory. Following the installation of the Catholic Visigoth Doge, Recardo (also known as Reccared), and his court at Itálica, the town was renamed "Bética" and the colonia of Córduba was rebranded with its present name.

The Visigoths were stigmatized by the Romans as savages who were as uncultured as they were vile, but in reality, the migratory group were vastly creative and architecturally competent. Their skills, for one, were embodied in the Basilica de San Vicente, or the St. Vincent Basilica, which was built over the demolished Roman temple by the Guadalquivir. One can still find the remains of the Visigothic church in the basement of the current Mosque-Cathedral. According to some chroniclers, the basilica was built to commemorate the conversion of King Recardo and his aristocracy, who shed their Arian beliefs to embrace their new "Trinitarian Christian" faiths.

St. Vincent of Saragossa, now the Protomartyr of Spain, was a revered deacon from two centuries prior. Along with Bishop Valerius, the selfless deacon was persecuted and arrested as the result of a violent purge of Christians, and while Valerius was eventually released and exiled, Vincent, who refused to renounce his faith, was ruthlessly tortured. The man was apparently grilled alive on top of a sizzling gridiron while his tormentors inserted rusty iron hooks into his flesh. His badly burned body was then tossed into a jail cell covered with a bed of shattered pottery fragments, but through it all, none of these unimaginable abuses could break the resilient Vincent, whose faith remained so admirably unswerving that it prompted at least one of the guards to convert to the Christian faith.

Thanks to the excavation work conducted by conservation architect Felix Hernandez on the Mosque-Cathedral in 1928, it is possible to better visualize the architectural features of the Visigothic basilica. Among the most striking remnants of the 5th century structure are the chevet apse (a semi-circular recess that housed the main altar) and the corroded remains of a water tank that was once connected to a baptistery pool. Another feature that intrigued Hernandez were the inscriptions he found etched onto the brick walls – "EX OFF [ICINA] LEONTI" – which identifies the 6th century workshop that provided the materials and craftsmanship. "Chrismons," more precisely Christograms depicting Christ's initials in Greek, were carved alongside these inscriptions.

The Aljama

"Your foundations are lasting,

Your columns countless,

Like the profusion of palms,

In the plains of Syria..." - Allama Muhammad Iqbal, "The Mosque of Cordoba" (1933)

In 711, Moorish forces from the Ummayad Caliphate poured into Córdoba, where they proceeded to uproot the Visigothic flags, and replace them with their own. It did not take long for the Iberian Peninsula to be rechristened "Al-Andalusia," otherwise known as "Islamic Spain," and within five years, Córdoba had been bumped up to the status of emirate under the Caliphate of Syrian Damascus.

Córdoba's port had always been a valuable and lucrative component to those who held the reins, but it was in the summer of 755, when Abd ar-Rahman I rose to power, that the city became a vibrant haven for intellectuals and religious scholars. As the she son of Umayyad prince Muawiya ibn Hisham and his Berber mistress, Rah, 24-year-old Abd ar-Rahman, like most royals of that age, lived in the lap of luxury, so much so that the scorned masses began to criticize the ruling dynasty's hypocrisy and demand change, to no avail. The public took issue with what they deemed to be the royals' shamelessly lavish lifestyle, but it was the authorities' unfair taxation of non-Arab Muslims and non-Muslims, as well as the other skewed policies that contradicted the Quran, that caused the greatest offense. Worse yet was the use of military force to suppress the voices of the public that was supposedly sanctioned by the Ummayad royals. And not only were the royals unfairly profiting from societal outcasts, they openly hunted, drank irresponsibly, and engaged in all sorts of anti-Islamic debauchery while posturing as religiously dutiful individuals.

In 750, Abu al-Abbas led a triumphant revolution against the Damascus-based Umayyad Caliphate and installed his new Abassid caliphate in Kufa. To ensure that there would be no attempt at reclaiming the throne, he set out to eliminate every last one of the adult Ummayads. Chroniclers estimate that up to 80 of the disgraced royals were deceived and executed in similar fashion. They were baited with amnesty and invited into Al-Abbas' quarters, where they unknowingly dined on their last suppers before being slain. 19-year-old ar-Rahman was one of the only ones who survived this purge.

With this target on his back, ar-Rahman packed up a small satchel and, accompanied by his former slave Badr, made the trying journey to North Africa in the hopes of shaking off his assassins. There, he tracked down the Nafzas – his mother's native tribe – and as he camped out amongst them, he outlined his political ambitions in Islamic Spain and sent Badr there to lay the foundations for his new base.

It was only on the 14th of August, 755 that ar-Rahman finally arrived at Almuñécar (in what is now the province of Granada). He was warmly welcomed by the Syrian immigrants and Umayyad royalists there who thirsted for change in Al-Andalusia. With the backing of his faithful adherents, ar-Rahman directed an effective insurgency that overthrew Yusuf al-Fihri, the last of the old-generation Umayyad governors of Islamic Spain. On the 15th of May the following year, he marched into Córdoba and was officially crowned emir in the grandest mosque there.

J. Conde, who authored the *History of the Dominion of the Arabs in Spain*, vividly described his arrival:"[Ar-Rahman] was himself at the time in the very flower of his youth; his deportment was graceful, his aspect noble and beautiful...his counteance at once friendly and majestic; he was of good stature, and his form was slight..."

The lively, glittering procession ar-Rahman was endowed with was nothing short of astounding, but the new emir, as they say, had exquisite tastes. The existing mosque was far too cramped and nondescript for his liking, so it was obviously deemed insufficient to honor the great Allah, who had guided him to his new throne.

Naturally, ar-Rahman spent the following years securing and expanding his territories. First and foremost, he tore down and completely rebuilt the Roman bulwarks that circled the city. He then purchased hordes of European and Berber slaves and put them to work as either laborers for his infrastructure projects or soldiers for his growing army. In an effort to prevent a repeat of the Umayyad dynasty's fate back in Damascus, the Córdoban emir made certain not to declare himself as "caliph," and he promoted a harmonious society in which Muslims, Jews, and Christians lived amicably alongside one another. And while the same heavy taxation on non-Muslims applied, the new emir appeared to be more liberal-minded than his predecessors, for he allowed certain "privileges" previously outlawed, such as the sale of (albeit taxed) alcohol to non-Muslims. Moreover, it is believed that the Christians and Muslims shared the Visigothic church with few if any complications.

Still, it is next to impossible to get a tiger to change his stripes, and while ar-Rahman threw plenty of sumptuous banquets and parties, he also spent generous amounts on rebuilding and piecing together new government buildings and public spaces. The brand-new buildings that were erected came furnished with gardens overflowing with fruits and vegetables both reminiscent of and directly imported from Syria.

Noel Walley's picture of a statue in Almuñécar depicting ar-Rahman

Ar-Rahman kept his vision for a grander mosque in the background as he strengthened the more vital parts of his kingdom, but by the time the 780s rolled around, bringing with it an influx of Muslim immigrants and converts, the emir felt he had to take action. In the spring of 784 or 785, shortly after the emir requisitioned the rebuilding of the old Alcázar, ar-Rahman purchased the Basilica of San Vicente from the Christian authorities, along with its surrounding land, for about 100,000 dinars. This would be the site of his new mosque, the Aljama, while the Christians, content with the compensation, used the money to build a new church on the outskirts of Córdoba.

The Aljama, the original name of the present Mosque-Cathedral, was most likely pushed forward to accommodate the fresh wave of Muslim immigrants, but some chroniclers claim it was a visit from an angel that compelled ar-Rahman to bring his original vision to fruition. As the story goes, late one evening, ar-Rahman was jolted awake from his slumber to find a spectral figure by the foot of his bed, bathed in a blinding golden glow. Without saying a word, the phantasm placed his hand on the trembling emir's shoulder, and at once, a terrible image flashed in his mind's eye as he watched his burning soul desperately paddle away from the devil, gasping for air as he struggled to keep afloat in a horrific sea of blood. When the apparition retracted his hand, ar-Rahman crumpled to the floor, crying out for mercy. It was only then that the angel told him to build a mosque over the Visigothic church, one worthy enough to atone for his sins and ensure his soul would be spared.

However it happened, Ar-Rahman was determined to raise the most majestic mosque in all of Al-Andalusia. The initial blueprints for the rectangular Aljama consisted of the following: a handsome walled sahn, or courtyard about 240 feet wide and 197 feet deep, followed by a vast "masjid" or prayer hall of similar dimensions that boasted 11 longitudinal aisles and a dozen bays. And while the bulk of the original basilica was knocked down, the emir opted to keep some of the original foundations, as well as a section of the Visigothic basement.

Jim Gordon's picture of the prayer hall

As the centerpiece of the Moorish sanctuary, the design and opulence of the prayer hall was ar-Rahman's primary focus. In an effort to maximize the plump budget they were provided, the architects recycled some of the original structures and materials. Several of the capitals, columns, and shafts used in the building of the Aljama were from the Roman and Visigothic eras, and some were directly shipped in from other parts of Spain, Europe, and North Africa. The distinctive hypostyle hall, which came with a flat roof ornamented with gold and brightly colored motifs, was shored up by dizzying arcades of pillars.

The horseshoe arches rested on a total of 1,293 columns (of which 856 are left intact) fashioned out of various precious stones, including onyx, jasper, marble, and granite. These unique arches were pieced together with alternating sandy-red and eggshell-white voussoirs (wedge-shaped stones used to form the curve of an arch), a color palette meant to echo an enchanting "forest of date palms." The use of these dual-toned voussoirs is a style often used in Damascus and Jerusalem, and the Moorish architects themselves lifted the style from the Romans, who were famous for embedding colored blocks of marble into their arches (though the arches of Aljama were made out of stone and brick instead).

Berthold Werner's picture of some of the columns

There were two levels of horseshoe arches within the new mosque, one on the bottom level and one on the upper level. The overlapping arches, which made for more elevated ceilings, were designed as such to allow for much as natural lighting from the courtyard as possible. Sunlight also trickled in from the four cupolas. In a bid to create a larger and more comfortable interior, the enterprising architects designed a new method of "two-tier construction by "using taller columns as a base, and planting shorter ones on top."

Curiously, the "orientation" of the mosque faced the south, as opposed to Mecca in the east, mirroring the orientation of the mosque in Damascus. Historians now believe that this was due to the location and placement of the Guadalquivir banks in the 8th century CE, which prevented them from orientating the mosque towards Mecca. As such, the mihrab, or prayer niche – then facing a stone wall garnished with intricate carvings of Quran verses and Islamic inscriptions – was situated in the southern wing of the Aljama.

Ingo Mehling's picture of the mihrab

Alonso de Mendoza's picture of the exterior

Unfortunately, ar-Rahman would not live to see the Aljama in its full glory, as he died two years later, but his son and successor, Hisham I of Córdoba, picked up from where the previous emir had left off. Among his most notable additions was the mosque's first minaret in the year 788. The minaret, known as the "Alminar Tower," was where Islamic worshipers convened 5 times a day, following the summoning of a "muezzin," or crier. As practiced since the time of the Prophet Muhammad, Muslims climbed up the spiral staircase to the top of the tower, a point that loomed over the rest of the mosque, to pay tribute to their deity. No blueprints of the early version of the Alminar Tower have survived, but historians believe the circular tower most likely resembled a narrow, multi-tiered cake with a protruding open-air balcony. Perched atop the cake-like tower was either a bulb-shaped dome or a "metal-covered cone," the upper levels of the tower painstakingly embellished with geometric carvings and Islamic verses.

Five years later, Hisham installed a network of galleries, as well as the mosque's first ablution well, a fountain within the courtyard of the Aljama, which he financed with 20% of the loot his forces swiped during their military campaigns against Narbonne and Gerona. Worshipers were expected to cleanse themselves in these pools, which measured about 460 feet in length and 280 feet in width, before prayer. Female worshipers then dried themselves off and proceeded to the sahn galleries, while the male worshipers headed off to the top of the Alminar. There, they prayed alongside one another on the cold, hard floor, patted down with "reddish slaked lime and sand." Slaves and laborers from Muslim, Jewish, and Christian backgrounds were employed for the project, as evidenced by their signatures on some of the bricks on the mosque's walls.

Word continued to spread about the oasis-like Islamic sanctuary at Córdoba, and as the population steadily soared, the city's emirs scrambled to expand existing structures and raise new buildings to cater to the new citizens.

In 822, Emir Abd Ar-Rahman II launched the first expansion of the Aljama. To begin with, the prayer hall swelled in size with the addition of the 8 new naves or "arcs" attached to the southern part of the mosque. To make room for the new naves, the qibla wall in the prayer niche and the Alminar Tower were razed down and rebuilt. Mohamed bin Abur Rahman I, who claimed the throne about three decades later, took charge of refurbishing the Puerta de San Esteban (Saint Esteban Gate) built by Ar-Rahman I.

Artencordoba describes Mohamed's addition in the following passage: "Through this door, one could access the prayer hall of the [Aljama]...It experienced a great remodeling in the time of Mohamed I, in the 9th century, who paid special attention to the construction of a new horseshoe arch, different to the previous one, and to the carving of decorative motifs, as well as the important inscriptions...The layout is similar in all the doors, with a lintelled alcove over which there is a blind horseshoe arch with alfiz. In this case, it is crowned by a stone rood supported by round modillions [sic] and, over it, there is a series of stepped battlement...An inscription in Kufic characters, which goes along the intrados of the arch and the horizontal higher part of the lintel, goes as follows: 'In the name of Allah, Most Graceful, Most Merciful. The Emir (blessed by Allah) Mohamed...commanded to build the...of this Mosque and its foundations (Allah's mercy be with him and accompany him). And it was completed...the year 241 (of the Hegira and 855 CE) with Allah's blessings and fortunate protection...'"

Upon the death of Emir Mohamed I in 886, his son, Al-Mundhir, inherited the torch. He reportedly ordered the production of a "bayt al-mal" ("Hall of Treasury"), which was deliberately made to hover over the first level, propped up by eight Corinthian capitals, to stave off thieves. The location of the secret passageway and entrance leading to the mosque's treasury, brimming with mounds of gold, silver, jewels, and other scintillating valuables, continues to stump historians to this day. Al-Mundhir also approved a string of renovations, including the modernization of the mosque's water canals, and the strengthening of its roof.

Al-Mundhir's son (or, according to some chroniclers, his brother), Abdullah ibn Mohamed al-Umawi, followed in his forerunner's footsteps. On top of the sabat, he ordered construction of a secret bridge that linked the emir's palace to the Alminar Tower. He was also the first to install a maqsura, or a private prayer space reserved for the emir.

In 929, Abd Ar-Rahman III was declared the first caliph of Córdoba. The caliph may have instituted the least number of changes and additions to the Aljama, but under his reign, the city was propelled to unprecedented heights, and its status as the beating heart and intellectual powerhouse of the Moors' kingdom in Spain was cemented.

Though the modifications he made paled in comparison to those that preceded and succeeded him, the alterations were significant all the same. First, the caliph tore down and rebuilt the increasingly lopsided Alminar Tower, and he slightly broadened the girth of the courtyard. The following excerpt, taken from the official website of the Mezquita, highlights the beauty of the new Alminar, its majesty supposedly so splendid it went on to inspire the future minarets that cropped up in Marrakesh, Rabat, and Seville: "Sources are unanimous about its monument nature and beauty. With a square floor plan, it was divided into 2 sections of different heights, structured around a central buttress from which came 2 staircases. The first of these had 4 windows with double horseshoe arches on its northern and southern facades, whereas the eastern and western faces had openings with 3 peepholes...The second body was open on all 4 sides and crowned with a gilded bronze dome on which the yamur was placed, the iron rod that finished off the structure..."

He also instructed the laborers to buttress the existing arches that tethered the prayer hall to the courtyard, which had begun to sprout cracks along the structures as a result of the weight of the naves. Finally, he had the builders raise an enormous horseshoe arch over the keyhole-shaped entrance connecting the mosque to the palace, and inserted a "semi-circular vault" between both buildings. The entrance was also bordered by stone tiles featuring a pattern of painted red diamonds. Furthermore, he polished up the facade of the prayer room suspended over the courtyard, a project documented in the inscriptions upon the Blessing Arch. In total, he mounted onto the facade 11 horseshoe arches braced by Corinthian capitals and slender columns with "rose-colored shafts."

Al-Hakam II was proclaimed the second caliph of Córdoba following the demise of his father, ar-Rahman III, in 961. Much like his father, 46-year-old al-Hakam was an ardent patron of the arts and sciences. He himself was superbly educated, having received extensive training in a variety of sciences and literature. Some accounts claim that al-Hakam possessed a whopping personal collection of over 600,000 books purchased from as far away as Damascus, Baghdad, Cairo, Medina, Constantinople, Kufa, and Basra, among others. Under his reign, thousands of Latin and Greek manuscripts were translated to Arabic, a laborious effort carried out by a caliph-appointed committee of Muladi Muslims and Mozarab Catholics. He was held in such high regard in the literary world that even Persian books written in the rival Abbasid dynasty honored him, and he was beloved by his subjects, Muslims and Christians alike.

With even more Muslim immigrants from near and far teeming into the colorful city, the Aljama, or as it was colloquially known to the Spanish citizens, the "Mezquita," was due for yet another expansion. Al-Hakam II's first order of business was to add another dozen naves to the prayer hall, with the end of the mosque inching closer and closer to the Guadalquivir. Unlike those who came before him, the caliph used new materials for his expansion, among them raw blocks of pink and blue marble. The qibla wall in the communal (but male-only) prayer niche was not only relocated, but reinforced to withstand the weight of the naves above it.

The caliph's maqsura, which faced the Alminar, was also augmented with new skylights, and further enhanced with Syrian-style motifs and gorgeous mosaics. Above the glinting, seemingly gold-plated double-door to the west of the mihrab was a horseshoe arch. There are golden Kufic inscriptions etched into the black of the marble that bordered the arch, and as seen in the panels above the other doors, another 6 square borders framed the arch. The 3rd and 5th panels were also decorated with the same golden inscriptions.

A special set of polylobed arches are found only in the maqsura in the stead of the usual horseshoes, each arch adorned with free-form wedges depicting exquisite carvings of vegetables, fruits, flowers, swirls, and other Moorish-friendly patterns. The uniqueness of these arches was intentional, to showcase its exclusivity. The marvelous domed roof of the maqsura featured a complex, but brilliant design – the ceiling of the dome appeared almost decagonal with the "star-ribbed" design in its center, one made to mimic the Islamic eight-pointed star, otherwise known as a "khatim," or "khatim-sulayman" (the seal of the prophets).

Nestled within the triangular gaps and crevices of the star-ribbed dome were panels completely covered with Byzantine-style tesserae, each shimmering shard glued on with "vitreous paste." The better part of the tiles were dipped in gold, but tiles in sable-black, chocolate-brown, mossy-green, and ruby-red were also used for the Arabesque floral and geometric patterns repeated throughout the dome. The dome of the maqsura was the mastermind of an unnamed but reputable Byzantine artisan, sent by the Byzantine court as a neighborly act of goodwill. The eight latticed windows encircling the section directly underneath the domed ceiling created mesmerizing crisscrossing shadows on the peach-tinted marble floors of the maqsura.

A Love Story for the Ages

"We are the most worthy to fulfil our right, and the most entitled to complete our good fortune, and to put on the clothing granted by the nobility of God, because of the favour which He has shown us, and the renown which He has given us, and the power to which He has raised us, because of what He has enabled us to acquire, and because of what He has made easy for us and for our state [? dynasty; Arabic: dawla] to achieve; He has made our name and the greatness of our power celebrated everywhere; and He has made the hopes of the worlds depend on us [Arabic: a'laqa], and made their errings turn again to us and their rejoicing at good news be (rejoicing at good news) about our dynasty [Arabic: dawla]. And praise be to God, possessed of grace and kindness, for the grace which He has shown, [God] most worthy of superiority for the superiority which He has granted us. We have decided that the da'wa should be to us as Commander of the Faithful and that letters emanating from us or coming to us should be [headed] in the same manner. Everyone who calls himself by this name apart from ourselves is arrogating it to himself [unlawfully] and trespassing upon it and is branded with something to which he has no right. We know that if we were to continue [allowing] the neglect of this duty which is owed to us in this matter then we should be forfeiting our right and neglecting our title, which is certain. So order the khaṭīb in your place to pronounce [the khuṭba] using [this title] and address your communications to us accordingly, if God will. Written on Thursday, 2 Dhū al-Ḥijja 316 [16 January 929]" - A letter proclaiming Abd ar-Rahman III's assumption of the caliphal title

Given what came before him, it would not be fair to say that Abd ar-Rahman III singlehandedly injected the grandeur into Cordoba. The southern Spanish city had already been a prestigious paragon of wealth and blended cultures, as well as an exemplar of advanced technology and creativity long before he was even conceived.

To begin with, the Moorish rulers of Cordoba displayed religious tolerance towards the traditionally rival faiths of Judaism and Christianity. Forced conversions were a rarity. Jewish and Christian scholars and engineers, for the most part, were granted close to equal opportunity to thrive. Moreover, while women were still leaps and bounds away from 21st century standards of equality, the women under the Ummayad Caliphate were granted certain rights and freedoms that were largely unheard of during this time. Women, albeit mostly those in the middle and upper echelons of society, were given the opportunity to learn reading and calligraphy, and they were permitted to certain areas of the workforce; most working women were appointed scribes at the Ummayad court.

The Ummayad Caliphate's enterprising celebration of unity allowed for the different elements within the mélange of cultures to shine, leading to accelerated growth and progress within the Cordoban community. Some of the city's most spectacular landmarks, such as the sublime Mezquita, rose during this period. While the rest of Europe struggled to escape the darkness of disunity and barbarism, out of Cordoba flashed a promising beam of light.

The inspiration and ingenuity that pervaded Cordoba also led to the works of various innovators. There was Abbas ibn Firnas, a 9th century inventor and overall polymath who dabbled in the fields of science, medicine, music, poetry, and more. Metronomes, water clocks, and a contraption that "simulated the motions of the cosmos" were just some of the pioneering inventions attributed to this Andalusian prodigy, who spent most of his life based in the Emirate of Cordoba. Firnas also developed one of the world's first flying machines; in 852, he strapped himself into a loose cloak fitted with wooden struts and jumped from the minaret of the city's grand Mezquita. He intended to sail through the skies like a hawk, only to fall nearly straight down. Fortunately, the cloak stalled his descent, acting as a parachute of sorts. He was evidently undeterred by this episode, for he tried again in 875 at the age of 70, this time diving off a mountaintop with eagle feathers stitched on a silk cloak.

Another luminary was Ali ibn-Nafi, also known as "Ziryab," or "Blackbird," an Iraqi native who relocated to Cordoba sometime in the mid-9th century. Ibn-Nafi was reportedly one of the first to introduce crystal glasses to Europe, and he also popularized the notion of a three-course meal, which consisted of soup, then a savory dish of meat or fish, followed by a lighter platter of assorted nuts and fruits.

That said, while Abd ar-Rahman III had inherited an already well-functioning empire, he certainly played an instrumental role in propelling his domains to even greater heights. Unlike his womanizer" of a father Muhammad ibn-Abdullah (son and first heir of Abdullah ibn Muhammad al-Umawi, 7th Emir of Cordoba), ar-Rahman III is often depicted in lore as something of a sensitive soul. As per tradition, ar-Rahman III wedded at least twice and engaged in his fair share of sexual affairs throughout his marriages. Joan Fallon, author of *The Shining City*, explains the comparably liberal attitude the Moors of Hispania had towards marriage and sex in an article entitled "Sexuality in Muslim Spain": "[Moorish Spain] promoted marriage and within marriage most forms of sexual activity were allowed...In [10th century] Al-Andalus, if you were part of the intellectual or political elite, your sexual practices were never questioned." Remarkably, homosexuality was greatly tolerated in Moorish Spain. Ar-Rahman III's son and future heir, Al-Hakam II, was reportedly openly bisexual.

A painting depicting ar-Rahman III and his court in the Medina Azahara

When ar-Rahman III fell, he fell hard, his eyes immovably riveted on his object of interest until the feelings that came flooding in dissipated, sometimes as quickly as they came. He was, as maintained by the chroniclers on his payroll, a man who knew not of the existence of barriers and limits, and he pursued whatever his heart desired with all of his being. It was all part of his magnetic charm.

That charm was paired with dashing good looks; his biographers describe him as a light-skinned individual with twinkling blue eyes and sharp features, though a bit shorter and stouter than average. In addition to dying his red hair jet-black, he was broad-shouldered, good-humored, and an excellent rider. What's more, he was a political wunderkind and a leader as competent as he was ambitious, which made his love story all the more idyllic.

Ar-Rahman III was no older than 22 when he was first crowned the Emir of Cordoba in 912. A liberal-minded, but zealously pious young adult, the powerful prince was nicknamed "Al-Nasir" by his subjects, meaning "Defender of the Faith." On the 16th of January, 929, the audacious ar-Rahman III detached himself from his allies, the Abbasid and Fatimid caliphates, as well as the Christian sovereigns of Leyn, and proclaimed himself the Caliph of Cordoba, a glittering title he held for the next three decades or so. Up until this point, his predecessors had settled upon the title of emir, while the caliphate remained under the control of the emperor, who presided over the hallowed territories of Mecca and Medina. Ar-Rahman III succeeded in seizing control of not only Iberia, but the Islamic territories in Africa, too.

The self-proclaimed caliph was, to many in Islamic Spain, a godsend. Following the consolidation of his power, he installed a streamlined, centralized government in Hispania. Additionally, he marshaled together one of the largest, and one of the most extensively trained navy fleets in the world. His court and subjects also lauded him for his economic savvy, as the imperial treasury alone contained more than 20 million gold pieces. Jewish courtier and imperial financier, Hasdai ibn-Shaprut, mentioned the empire's annual revenues: "The revenue of [Abd ar-Rahman III] amounts annually to 100,000 florins, this arising only from the income derived from numerous merchants who come hither from various countries and isles... The kings of the world no sooner perceive of the greatness of my monarch, than they hasten to convey to him presents in abundance..."

As is usually the case with transitions in power, ar-Rahman III initially received some push-back from his freshly acquired subjects, but his high-reaching endeavors soon appeased even his most vocal critics. Ar-Rahman III understood that the continued promotion of unity was key to his success, and as such, preserved the atmosphere of tolerance upheld by his forerunners. He bettered the balance between religion, science, and the arts, and ensured that a uniform amount of attention was placed upon each sphere.

The charismatic caliph was also greatly skilled in utilizing the different strengths and aspects to his character to better appeal to his varied underlings. To prevail upon the intellectuals of Cordoban society, ar-Rahman III showed off his knowledge of literature, religious texts, and the various sciences. He disarmed the commoners of his empire by abolishing the numerous taxes irrelevant to Sharia law, which had previously been used to accommodate the luxurious whims of the former emirs. He was exceptionally lenient with rebels and traditionalists, offering them amnesty as a way to coax them to his side.

At the end of the day, it was ar-Rahman III's dedication to the enhancement of public infrastructure and local industries, as well as his determination to revive the religious spirit of Cordoba that sealed the deal. There were more than 3,000 mosques and close to 100,000 shops, eateries, and local establishments in Cordoba alone during ar-Rahman III's tenure. The caliph's vigorous advocacy for education further cemented Cordoba as the home of Europe's most enlightened intellectuals. As the 19th century Arabic scholar Reinhart Dozy put it, "Nearly everyone [in Cordoba and the Al-Andalus] could read and write...whilst in Christian Europe, only rudiments of learning were known, and that by the few, mostly clergy." Earning the trust of his subjects, many say, was a critical part of the Medina Azahara's almost impossibly expeditious construction process.

Contemporary writers claim that just three years after ar-Rahman III declared himself caliph, the intrepid soul stumbled head over heels in love like he had never before in all his 41 years. It was for her that he took on what would be the magnum opus of not only his career, but a sparkling monument that intended to encapsulate and honor the undying legacy of the Al-Andalusian emirs and caliphs.

To ar-Rahman III, an enthusiastic patron of culture and the arts, money was of little concern, but while he was nowhere near a frugal king, he spent wisely. As reported by the Britannica, "a third of ar-Rahman III's revenue sufficed for the ordinary expenses of government, a third was hoarded, and a third spent on buildings." Needless to say, when it came to his beloved, money was not at all an issue.

It was not the lavishness of the complex, nor the fact that this formidable character built it for no other reason than love that many find most intriguing. Instead, people are typically amazed at who the caliph's true love was. Despite ar-Rahman III's apparently tender nature, 13th century Moroccan author Ibn Idhari claimed that the caliph's personal harem consisted of 6,300 concubines of differing races, nationalities, and backgrounds. There were three levels in the hierarchy of women in ar-Rahman III's palace. Perched at the top was the queen matriarch and director of the harem, ar-Rahman III's Christian mother, Muzna. Next was the caliph's queen consort, Murjan, the wife who produced for him his male heir, al-Hakam II. Following Murjan was Fatima bint al-Mundhir, along with the rest of his wives and mothers of his other children.

The queen matriarch and consorts dwelt in similar laps of luxury, and not only enjoyed all the amenities of the palace, but were allowed to come and go as they pleased. The concubines and slaves of ar-Rahman III's palace were afforded no such luxury, as even the caliph's favorite concubines had to first acquire permission from the queen matriarch.

Justo José Moreno Mérida's picture of a statue depicting Al-Hakam II

The concubines of Moorish Spain were certainly regarded as commodities, but they received opportunities that many would have been deprived of otherwise. Concubines were made to attend harem school, where, in addition to lessons pertaining to the erotic arts, the ladies were trained to read, write, and expand on a number of artistic and creative skills, such as dancing, singing, and poetry recitals. Each woman was also expected to learn at least one type of musical instrument.

Owing to the immensity of ar-Rahman III's harem, the ladies actually summoned by the caliph comprised only a small sliver of his sexual entourage. The caliph's attention was coveted by many, if not most of the women in his harem, for being promoted to one of ar-Rahman III's favorites meant a hefty salary and an opulent, fully furnished room in the palace, amongst other "privileges."

Writers from the era asserted that Az-Zahra, the ravishing young maiden who snagged and held the attention of ar-Rahman III like no other, first caught his interest when she made her debut on the caliph's private stage. Garbed in a two-toned, beautifully embroidered dress that flowed down to her ankles and a lovely headscarf to match, the captivating concubine shimmied towards the wonderstruck caliph. She was not the headliner – in fact, she was no more than a background dancer - but it seemed as if the spotlight only shined down upon her. He straightened up in his seat at once as he gazed upon her delicate, yet striking features, her movements made even more entrancing by the shimmering bangles on her arms.

As recounted by the Andalusian poet, Isner, it appeared as if those in the caliph's cortege had taken notice of Az-Zahra, too. Ibn Arabi, one of ar-Rahman III's courtiers, nudged the caliph. "My lord," Arabi muttered hoarsely. "Do you see the beauty of this beautiful slave?" To this, the distracted ar-Rahman III said nothing, his unblinking gaze glued to the graceful dancer before him. There was his answer.

Following the dance, ar-Rahman III made a beeline for Az-Zahra, and invited her to spend the evening with him. And thus began the most fervid and impassioned love story of all time. Ar-Rahman III's love for Az-Zahra soon eclipsed his feelings for Murjan and Fatima, so much so that his consorts became deeply envious when it dawned on them that the concubine was more than just the caliph's temporary preference. Az-Zahra, as the legend goes, was at once awarded the finest and most spacious room in the palace.

Much to ar-Rahman III's dismay, the enchanting concubine was tortured by an inexplicable sadness that even the most sumptuous feasts and dozens of ladies-in-waiting could not fix. Now on a quest to eliminate the sorrow that was eating away at his beloved, ar-Rahman III ordered the construction of the largest and most brilliantly resplendent palace-city in all the region. In 936, the caliph organized a construction team made up of the most illustrious architects and artisans in his empire. The princely palace-city was to resemble a paradise on earth.

To complete this vision, the blocks of marble, stone tiles, and even the boulders and rubble used to construct the buildings of the palace-city were imported from faraway lands, and the most trivial materials were inspected and tossed out if they failed to pass quality control. The divinely colorful gardens planted within the walls of the premises were filled with a variety of exotic trees and flowers, and inhabited by sweet songbirds and charming critters. More transfixing yet were the gorgeous interiors of the newly erected monuments, though they paled in comparison to the mesmerizing, sprawling residence of ar-Rahman III and Az-Zahra. The walls were embellished with intricate geometric patterns and designs hand-painted by the most skilled artists in the land. Rooms were hung with festoons of brightly-colored silks and fabrics, as well as radiant flowers replaced on a daily basis. To say that the palace oozed grandeur would be a severe understatement; even the floors of this fantastic castle were reportedly tiled with bars of gold.

When all was said and done, a positively giddy ar-Rahman III returned to Az-Zahra, desperately seeking even a trace of a genuine smile on her face. Indeed, Az-Zahra humored the caliph with one, but the disappointed ar-Rahman III knew he had yet again fallen short of his objective. He insisted for his beloved to disclose to him what it would take for her heart to be wholly content.

Az-Zahra was initially hesitant, perhaps not wanting to appear unappreciative of this grand gesture of cosmic proportions, but the caliph continued to press her until she relented. It is not difficult to imagine why the concept of complete and wholehearted happiness would be so foreign to a woman in Az-Zahra's position, one with a predetermined fate and slim to no chances of exploring her full potential. The young girl, a native of Granada, was born into extreme poverty and sold as a sexual object by her own grandfather as a teenager. Az-Zahra, unbearably homesick, yearned to relive the short-lived innocence of her youth, and she found herself longing for the simple, but tenderly nostalgic parts of her childhood. Above all, she revealed to ar-Rahman III, she wished to see the lace-white blankets of snow that dusted the crests of the Sierra Nevada Mountains. Other versions of the story identify Az-Zahra as a native of Syria, and the Sierra Nevada Mountains as an unspecified range in Syria.

The following day, ar-Rahman III arranged for them to embark on a trip down south to Granada. Sure enough, it was during this impromptu getaway that the caliph witnessed the authentic smile he had been looking for all this time. He knew precisely what to do next. In an effort to allow Az-Zahra to experience this joy year-round – and for the rest of her days – the caliph rounded up his men and demanded that they execute the inconceivable task of tearing down a vast chunk of the towering "black mountain" (Sierra Morena) darkening the palace with its shadow. Naturally, a few of his advisers protested against destroying what they thought to be a gift from Allah, but ar-Rahman III remained firm. The caliph replied indignantly, "Allah does not allow the Prince of Believers to think of something that disgusts reason just by hearing it! If all the creatures were brought together during the whole life in this world digging and cutting, I would not be able to eliminate it; I would not make it disappear more than the one who created it!"

When it became clear that there was no changing ar-Rahman III's mind, his men did as they were told, apparently completing the task within months. Shams, an elderly gardener with an unparalleled green thumb, was then brought into the equation. Under his instruction, ar-Rahman III's laborers planted hundreds upon hundreds of rows of Murcian almond and cherry trees on the flatland, as well as in all the gardens of ar-Rahman III's palace. It was a truly magical sight, and the pristine, fluffy white blossoms that sprouted from these elegant, slender-branched trees created the illusion of freshly fallen snow. In other versions of this tale, the obstruction was identified as a patch of dense, overgrown forestland instead of a "black mountain."

Whatever the case, it was thanks to ar-Rahman III's addition of the illusory winter wonderland that the light in Az-Zahra's life was finally rediscovered. Az-Zahra spent the rest of her days drifting about in the palace-city's multiple gardens, trimming and tending to the white-blossom trees. The caliph's heart, as one might expect, was irreparably shattered upon the inevitable death of Az-Zahra some decades later. As a final homage to the one true love of his life, he commissioned a group of sculptors to raise an exquisitely carved effigy featuring her likeness by the entrance of the palace-city. He then installed another 3,000 ivory and ebony columns throughout the Medina Azahara, and each pillar was encrusted with gold, jewels, and other precious stones, yet another symbol of his eternal love for her.

A Palace-City to Rival the Kingdom of God

"I have recalled you with longing in al-Zahra,

Between limpid horizon and sweet face of earth

Whilst the breeze languished at sunset,

Almost diseased with pity for me..." – Ibn Zaidun, 11th century poet

Perhaps not surprisingly, the love story behind the Medina Azahara, while certainly guaranteed to sweep romantics off their feet, has been branded fictitious by modern historians. There are some, for instance, who link the origins of the palace-city with the venerable Moorish scientist and inventor Abu al-Qasim al-Zahrawi. Known as "Abulcasis," he was at one point in time praised as the "greatest surgeon of the Middle Ages." Al-Zahrawi, they argue, was not simply the *archiater*, or "chief physician" of ar-Rahman III's court. Over time, he became one of the caliph's dearest friends.

On top of his numerous inventions, which included the catgut and a predecessor to modern-day forceps, the medical pioneer authored *Kitab al-Tasrif*, an all-encompassing encyclopedia more than 1,500 pages long. The compendium featured an in-depth look at 325 illnesses, as well as illustrations and thorough descriptions of 200 surgical instruments. The work was the first of its kind to dedicate an entire section to surgery, 300 pages in total. Ar-Rahman III, they say, was so impressed by the lasting impact al-Zahwari made in the field of medicine that he believed the man to be deserving of such an honor.

Although ar-Rahman III most likely erected a statue or monument of some sort as a tribute to al-Zahwari, experts assert that it is highly unlikely that the jewel of ar-Rahman III's empire would be named after him. To better understand the true origins of the splendid palace-city, historians believe it's necessary to deconstruct its name. Though a relatively common name during the time, Az-Zahra doubled as the Arabic term for "shine" or "brilliance," while "*madinat*" is the word for "city." Experts doubt that there ever was a single muse behind the Medina Azahara, and that its name was no more than a concise description of the hybrid city palace as the Shining City.

That said, thanks to the plethora of eyewitness accounts and the personal journal entries of visiting travelers throughout the years, it is difficult to remain skeptical about the magnitude of the medina's splendor. Of course, one must take into consideration the ancient chroniclers' tendency to exaggerate when it comes to the accomplishments of their infallible kings, but the large quantity of existing books, poems, and diary entries regarding the event is enough to convince historians not only of the palace-city's existence, but the great degree of its grandeur.

As for why ar-Rahman III chose to construct the medina in the first place, the majority of historians today have likened it to a political grandstanding of sorts. In addition to being a remarkable showcasing of his abilities and the talents of his subjects, it was intended to affirm the supremacy of his self-established caliphate. With this "Versailles of the Al-Andalus and the Middle Ages," he expected the veneration and unswerving loyalty of all his subjects, not just the inhabitants of Moorish Spain, but the Moorish territories in Baghdad and northern Africa, too. This adulation, experts agree, is what ar-Rahman III ultimately achieved. Antonio Vallejo, the chief archaeologist for one of the city's multiple excavations in recent years, explained that it "was the largest city ever built from scratch in Western Europe. Most large Western cities grow over time. This was built in a single effort, from a single design."

Ar-Rahman III was as devout of a Muslim as they came, but he was also immensely perceptive. Though he worked laboriously to weave Islam back into the mainstream, he had no delusions about the fact that 10th century aristocrats were far more concerned with money and material pomp than they were with adhering to the Holy Qu'ran. Indeed, the more educated one was, the more likely one was to scale the social ladder, but at a time when intellect was accessible to even the most common of men, "tribal affiliation" and the magnificence of one's property became determining factors that aided in boosting their status.

Ar-Rahman III was immediately confronted by two imposing hurdles when he declared himself caliph. The first was rooted in the self-governing (and thereby potentially rebellious) Moorish territory in Toledo, and the second problem involved the rival Fatimids, who openly flaunted their desire for the prosperous Spanish lands. The wave of intruders from North Africa, which came pouring in during the previous decades, was what led to the deterioration of a single, unified power in Moorish Spain in the first place. Those who triumphed in their conquests unpacked their warships in the seized provinces and proceeded to plant their flags there, and the tribal chiefs who ordered these invasions crowned themselves the emirs of these captured provinces. The Zul Nun made their home in Toledo, the Bani Hud stayed in Saragossa, the

Berbers were in Granada, the Banu Abbad were in Seville, and the Eastern European Slavs were in Valencia.

The fractured power structure in Moorish Spain would have intimidated most other monarchs, but the fearless ar-Rahman III remained unfazed. It soon became clear that ar-Rahman III was an excellent strategist, and his peerless diplomatic skills were incontestable, for slowly, but surely, he succeeded in retrieving these territories, squashing the attempted rebellions and eventually securing the allegiance and support of these tribes. The first phase of ar-Rahman III's internal conquest of Moorish Spain brought the recovery of Bobastro, Badejoz, Zamorra, Simancas, Osma, and Toledo, seemingly in one fell swoop. Next, he tackled the Christian territories in the northern half of Spain, in part as retaliation to the numerous raids and pillages they allegedly inflicted upon the fringes of Moorish domains. His attacks on Christian soil are said to have been so vicious that the regions of Castile, Navarre, Leon, Alva, and Galicia swiftly surrendered and even agreed to cough up annual tributes to Cordoba.

The Fatimids, however, who have virtually conquered all of North Africa, posed a more serious threat. They had gained a dedicated following of believers who were adamant in bowing only before the dynasty spawned by 8th century sovereign Imam Ismail ibn Jafar. The notorious lineage, feared even by the Ummayads in Cordoba and the Abbasids in Baghdad, had just usurped the Idrises, the former rulers of Algeria and Morocco, and had now set their sights on Spain. When Umar bin Hafsun, a recent Christian convert and vocal insurgent against the Ummayads, learned of these rumors, the calculating rogue approached both the Fatimids and his Christian brothers in the north and proposed a joint ambush on ar-Rahman III's territories. Embittered by the caliph's successes and resentful of his prowess in the battlefield, both parties soon signed off in agreement. Weeks later, an armed fleet of war vessels were dispatched to the southern Iberian coast, courtesy of the Fatimids.

Much to the conspirators' chagrin, it appeared that the insightful ar-Rahman III had anticipated the pitfall. Midway into their expedition, the Fatimids' warships were waylaid, ferociously assailed, and almost all sunk by the vessels of ar-Rahman III's unbeatable navy. The unstoppable caliph went on to lay siege to at least 70 of Umar's castles and bases. When Umar learned that his plan had unraveled, he attempted to flee, but he was chased down and apprehended by ar-Rahman III's men somewhere in the mountains of eastern Spain.

Umar fell to his knees and begged for ar-Rahman III's forgiveness in the spring of 915. Taking pity on the groveling, failed revolutionary, the merciful caliph granted him a full pardon, and as a gesture of goodwill, even allowed him to lord over a small province. The domains Umar previously presided over submitted to their new Moorish overlord with little resistance. This excerpt from Mario Telò's *European Union and New Regionalism* sums up the exchange: "[Umar] humbly submitted to [ar-Rahman III] and requested that he might be spared, with his permission, and that he may be [recognized] governor under his suzerainty in exchange for his payment of the land tax out of the tribute."

At this stage, ar-Rahman III had proven himself to be a proficient commander, both on the battle front and whilst seated upon the throne. At the same time, he exhibited Islamic compassion often unheard of in such power-starved sovereigns. This softened his image in the eyes of his subjects, who now viewed him as a true defender of the faith, one who spared the lives of rebels and mutineers provided that they play by his rules. The Medina Azahara, built decades later later, was akin to posturing, built to serve as a symbol of his dominance and superiority over all the Moorish terrains; it was, furthermore, an arresting reminder to all potential trespassers and marauders that his invulnerable record had yet to be broken. Umar, they say, was among the last to test the unshakable caliph.

Owing to the great antiquity of the palace-city, the year that construction commenced is still a matter of dispute, with some listing it as 936 and others as 940 CE. As previously mentioned, historians and archaeologists alike believe that the entire city, situated about 5 miles west of central Cordoba, was based off only a single set of blueprints, meaning the medina's size and its dimensions remained largely unaltered throughout the entire process. The provisional defensive walls that cordoned off the enormous rectangular complex measured about 5,000 feet long, paired with a width of about 2,500 feet. The dizzying compound contained 112 hectares of land, roughly the size of 113 international rugby fields.

Given its colossal dimensions, one would assume that tens of thousands, or perhaps even hundreds, were required to realize ar-Rahman III's tremendous vision, but chroniclers assert that only 10,000 to 15,000 men were employed, laying about 6,000 stone blocks a day. This was just half of the manpower utilized in the building of the Taj Mahal, a complex that measured about 1,900 feet in length and 1,000 feet in width – a true testament to the expertise and ingenuity of the medina's architects. More than 4,000 slender columns fashioned out of jasper and untouched marble blocks in varying shades of coral, white, and green shipped all the way from Phoenician Carthage were installed throughout the complex. These columns were each fitted with distinctive capitals with Byzantine and Corinthian undertones and embellished with complicated geometric patterns, as well as carvings of foliage.

The location of the medina was not chosen on impulse. Ar-Rahman III's architects capitalized on the diverse topography of the region, an intersection of the Sierra Morena and the Guadalquivir Valley, which allowed for a "terraced system" split into three tiers. The highest level of the medina was reserved only for the caliph and the royal courtrooms, and the remaining two levels were inhabited by the administrators and commoners, respectively.

There were three bridges that provided access to the palatial medina: the Nogales Bridge; the Bridge of Caño de María Ruiz; and the Bridge-Aqueduct of Valdepuentes. The bridge-aqueduct played perhaps the most instrumental role out of all three structures, since it was a remodeling of an existing Roman aqueduct built in the 1st century CE, which ran from the Sierra Morena to Cordoba. As the original artificial conduit lay several feet below the construction site of the medina, additional channels were attached so as to provide water for the second and uppermost levels. The traces of food, as well as ceramic remnants unearthed in these channels, reveal that a section of the original aqueduct was converted into the medina's main sewer. The multiple conduits tacked onto the unusually advanced sewage system had the ability to collect and conserve rainwater, as well as store waste water in separate repositories, which were regularly emptied.

The better part of the medina's monuments were mainly constructed out of sandstone and ashlar blocks similar to the building materials used in the capital's grand mezquita. They were most likely locally sourced from the Santa Ana de Albeida quarries just a few miles north of Cordoba, as were most of the other structures established by ar-Rahman III. The materials used in the ornamentation of the medina's monuments, on the other hand, were mostly imported, such as the aforementioned Phoenician marble. White marble was also shipped in from Estremoz in Portugal.

In traditional Moorish fashion, ar-Rahman III's architects incorporated calligraphic inscriptions of Qu'ran verses, as well as odes to the ruling caliph in the mosque, the palace, residential buildings, and public structures alike. Upon completing their projects, the architects etched their names onto the facade or some other prominent feature of the building, as an artist would their painting.

Marble was not only used in the columns shoring up the medina's innumerable arches; these smoothened slabs of crystallized limestone were also used to tile the floors of the palace-city's most glamorous rooms. In certain parts of ar-Rahman III's palace, as well as select rooms in his courthouses, a special type of domestically purchased purple limestone, known as "coquina," was used to pave the floors. The almost luminous stone, when struck by sunlight at the right angle, turned to dancing shades of violet, mulberry, and wine-red. The coquina-tiled floors were especially marvelous when enclosed by white stuccoed walls with black and crimson Arabesques.

The placement of the manifold facilities of the Medina Azahara, which contained labyrinthine arcades, keyhole-shaped arches, verdant gardens, glistening pools, and buildings of varying sizes and heights, to name a few, was meticulously planned beforehand. The Dar al-Mulk, ar-Rahman III's palace and the centerpiece of the medina, was built on the uppermost tier overlooking the rest of the medina, complete with a panoramic view of the compound's surrounding flatland and river, to represent the caliph's mastery over the Al-Andalus, all the Moorish territories, and the rest of Christian Europe. Only two other structures were worthy of being raised next to the Dar al-Mulk. The first was a regal estate for his firstborn and future heir, Al-Hakam II, and the second was a smaller, but similarly striking manor for his right-hand man, a bureaucratic eunuch by the name of Jafar al-Siqlabi. Ar-Rahman III's other children, who shied away from politics, resided in central Cordoba.

The level below the Dar al-Mulk was home to a series of courthouses, governmental buildings, and a few private residences for respected dignitaries and high-ranking officials in the caliph's retinue. Among the most impressive of these private residences was one that belonged to soon-to-be appointed Prime Minister Jafar al-Mushafi, who would later serve as regent on the behalf of the young Al-Hakam II. This patrician tier, though not quite as grandiose as the structures on the level above it, was still comfortably luxurious, so as to suit the tastes of the blue-blooded individuals that dwelt in these parts. Visitors would also find a few buildings that served as conference halls and venues for entertainment, two of them being the caliph's principal reception room, as well as the Dar al-Quzara, otherwise known as the "House of Viziers."

The lowest level of the Medina Azahara, which housed the royal infantry and cavalry barracks, as well as markets, baths, and compact residential complexes for plebeians, has yet to be excavated. As such, little information can be gathered about the appearance of these buildings. Scholars can only presume that these were more rustic in their facades and plainer in their adornments, but having said that, these structures and amenities were most likely as durable and as regularly maintained as their counterparts in the above tiers if they were to be permitted inside the caliph's precious Shining City.

An Unexcelled Show of Prestige

"...Its brilliance gives light like lamps to one traveling in the dark.

She is a pearl hidden in a shell...

A pearl for which Thought dives and remains unceasingly in the deeps of that ocean.

He who looks upon her deems her to be a gazelle of the sand-hills..." - Muhyyeddin Ibn Arabi, 12th century poet

Though the construction of the medina would not be completed until 976, ar-Rahman III moved in as early as 941. By then, most of the caliph's palace, as well as the medina's Mezquita Aljama, had already been installed.

A picture of the ruins of the Mezquita Aljama

Anyone privileged enough to set foot in the caliph's stupendous home found it almost impossible to believe that no more than five years had passed since its inception. The surrealism of the descriptions attached to the medina's palace provide only a glimpse of the alcazar's majesty. This poetic passage lifted from Joan Fallon's *The Shining City* described the scene: "Possibly his concubine glittered and shone with all the jewels and beautiful skills he showered upon her, but then so did the city...When visitors entered through the Grand Portico, passing beneath its enormous, red and white arches, when they climbed the ramped streets that were paved with blocks of dark mountain stone, passing the lines of uniformed guards in their scarlet jackets and the richly robed civil servants that flanked their way, when they reached the royal residence and saw the golden inlay on the ceilings, the marble pillars, the richly woven rugs scattered across the floors and the brilliant silk tapestries...then they indeed knew that they were in the Shining City..."

A picture of the portico

A picture of the upper basilica hall

Denyse Lamprière, a contributor to the *Andalucia* magazine and website, noted, "Bronze griffins, lions, and horses pour mountain water into thousands of marble fountains. In the shade of cypresses and palm trees and around huge reception halls, dream gardens form multi-colored carpets, mixing myrtle and rosemary, oleanders and tuberoses, lilies and roses. From the caliph's palace...the view extends over the whole Wadi al-Kabir Valley, and in the far distance, five kilometers to the east, the large city of Cordoba can be seen..."

Though most historians have now reduced the winking floors of pure gold, supposedly covering every square inch of the palace, to nothing more than a colorful element of a riveting myth, several accounts have made references to a mystical pool of mercury in the center of the caliph's reception hall, dubbed the "Salon Rico." The basin of this decorative fountain brimmed with thick, mirror-like quicksilver. During important celebrations and visits from notable figures, local and foreign, the welcoming committee shook the basin from side to side, which allowed the beam of sunlight shining onto the mercury to cast flickering specks of gold onto the marble walls and gold ceilings. This glimmering effect is said to have been so dazzling that it was reminiscent to many of lightning, which often startled ar-Rahman III's unsuspecting guests.

The Salon Rico was considered by many the most spellbinding part of the caliph's palace. The sumptuousness of the hall's lavishly decorated interior, built between the years 953 and 957, was what earned it its moniker, which translates into "Rich Hall."

The following entry, authored by 12th century scholar and geographer al-Zuhri, suggests the name didn't do justice to its full opulence: "Its roof was gold and thick with pure glass, as well as its walls; his tiles were of gold and silver. In the center...a pond full of mercury, and on each side of the room, eight doors opened, formed by ivory and ebony arches that rested on columns of colored glass, so that the rays of the sun, when entering through those doors, were reflected in its roof and its walls, producing...a blinding light...so that...[guests] were under the impression that the room was spinning in the air while the mercury was still moving...Some say that the room turned to face the sun, following its course, while others say it was fixed, without moving around the pond. No other sovereign, neither among the infidels nor in Islam, had built anything like it before, but it was possible for him to do so because of the abundance of mercury they had there..."

Many of the excavations in recent years have, in large part, revolved around the recovery of the marble pillars and glass walls in the Salon Rico. The same excavations aimed at uncovering the spandrels, the semi-triangular panels that fill the unused spaces of the horseshoe arches in the reception hall. Artisans painstakingly carved stylized, swirl-based patterns of trees, flowers, and other foliage known as "ataurique" onto these wedges. One spandrel recovered featured a fruit tree with multiple branches, captured in varying shapes and swirls, which experts believe symbolizes the "*Shajarat al-Kholoud*," or the Tree of Immortality in Islam.

Rob Ven's picture of an Arabesque panel

The eastern corner of the Rich Hall was partitioned off, further split into private rooms for ar-Rahman III and the future caliphs. One could enter through the Patio de la Pila, which provided different paths to the royal latrine, as well as other rooms of leisure. It was in these rooms that ar-Rahman III reportedly spent most of his downtime, often accompanied by a pile of books or some kind of puzzle.

There were at least three royal gardens in the medina, the most magnificent being the the "Prince's Garden." This "formal" garden, supposedly the oldest of its kind in all of Spain, measured about 66 feet in length and 62 feet across, with pavilions located on the east and west, a covered staircase that led to an upper level walkway on the north, and a marble wall on the southern end. An elegant fountain stood in the center of the greenery, connected to channels specially constructed to water the dozens upon dozens of flowerbeds.

The water that flowed through these channels was derived from the medina's bridge-aqueduct; water trickled out of small outlets punched into the marble and rained down upon the plants like clockwork. The vibrant collection of flowers in this particular garden included "roses, white and yellow jasmine, yellow narcissi, musk roses, wallflowers, violets, orleanders, anemones, and lilies." The royals and nobles spent much of their afternoons ambling about the upper level walkway, dreamily gazing down upon the "colorful carpet of flowers" below them.

Rabbits, squirrels, and other woodland creatures, which scurried freely throughout these gardens, were neighbors to numerous other animals from foreign lands, such as peacocks, pheasants, and even domesticated tigers, lions, and camels. Sculptures of animals, hewn from pure marble, bronze, silver, amber, and pearls, were mounted onto multi-tiered fountains, or installed as stand-alone works of art throughout the medina's gardens.

The presence of these animal statues is noteworthy in itself. Traditionally speaking, Moorish artists avoided human and animal depictions in their work. As this passage from an article published by the *Metropolitan Museum of Art* in October of 2001 explains, "The Islamic resistance to the representation of living beings ultimately stems from the belief that the creation of living forms is unique to God, and it is for this reason that the role of images and image makers has been controversial. The strongest statements on the subject...are made in the Hadith (Traditions of the Prophet), where painters are challenged to 'breathe life' into their creations and [are] threatened with punishment on the Day of Judgment."

While the Qu'ran is more vague when it comes to figurative depiction, it clearly condemns idolatry, an unforgivable violation known to the Moors as a "*shirk*." Ar-Rahman III, a known patron of the arts, was among the first to justify the use of animal representation in his medina, for these effigies were to be used solely as decorative pieces. Even so, the caliph made certain to tread lightly, instructing the sculptors on his payroll to produce only minimalistic, heavily stylized animal forms.

Lions, camels, hunting dogs, wolves, and other important animals in Islam were among some of the creatures featured on the tapestries, carvings, and statues of the medina. A handful of mythological beings that predated the faith, such as griffins (a creature with the head and animals of an eagle and the body of a lion) and harpies (creatures with the head and upper torso of an entrancing siren and the body of a bird), could also be found in the medina, among the many multicultural elements of the medina's architecture. The most compelling component of the gardens' amber animals, however, consisted of the silver birds perched upon handmade gilded trees, each fitted with mechanical devices that allowed them to emit melodious "chirps." As the medina's royal gardens abounded with both perishable and artistic treasures, thousands of armed soldiers and slaves guarded these enclosures around the clock.

The two remaining principal gardens were located in the middle and lowest terraces of the medina, one of which led to the Salon Rico. Located in the eastern wing of the medina, the latter garden was divided into four "sunken" quadrants to allow for better irrigation. It was decked out with rows of fruit trees and flowerbeds, as well as a quartet of rectangular pools in its center. The water that nourished the plant life on these four quadrants was derived from the channels that ran along the network of walkways.

It was only logical for a sovereign as devout as ar-Rahman III to dedicate extra time to perfecting the medina's mosque. The Mezquita Aljama, which lay in either the middle or lower level of the medina, was a stately, two-story structure assembled by at least 1,000 laborers and craftsmen. The immensity of the manpower, as well as the prowess and artistry of those involved, resulted in its "record completion," a period of 48 days.

Unfortunately, only scant descriptions of the mosque have survived the test of time, but experts believe it most likely resembled the more deluxe mosques of the city. The complex was probably square or quadrangular in shape, complete with a mihrab, a qibla wall, an ablution courtyard, topped with a minaret. The upper level of the mosque was most likely propped up by arcades and horseshoe, or keyhole-shaped arches with red-and-white striped voussoirs, and the temple adorned with geometric and stylized carvings of foliage, as per the traditional laws of Islam.

The serenity that impregnated the picturesque gardens of the medina was supposedly so potent that it remained long after the city crumbled. Royals and nobles often hiked up to the ruins of these parts for midday picnics and whatnot. One such royal was the Abbadid taifa of Seville, Al-Mu'tamid ibn Abbad, who embarked on one of these excursions with a small circle of companions in the summer of 1069. One of Abbad's courtiers logged the day's events in his journal later that day: "[We] climbed the high [ruins of the palatial] rooms...[We] sat on spring carpets covered with flowers...[We] drank wine glasses and walked around the place, enjoying, but also reflecting on life..."

Visiting ambassadors, delegates, and dignitaries were welcomed with quite the spectacle, to say the least. The path he took during the five-mile trek from Cordoba to the Medina Azahara, recounts an unnamed chronicler, was completely carpeted, the embroidered rugs colored in bright yellows and royal reds. Both sides of this carpeted path were lined with hundreds of the most beautiful young maidens in Cordoba, many of them from ar-Rahman III's personal harem. In one hand, they carried parasols that shielded their pretty faces from the glaring rays of the sun, and in the other, a silver platter of various refreshments for the passing traveler and his entourage.

This was not the end of the spectacular display. The visitors were then escorted through the "triumphal" gate on the east entrance of the medina. Once the lovely ivory doors of the *puerta* swung open, a band of soldiers and servants, clothed in their finest attire, marched them up to the Salon Rico. They were then brought to a room in the easternmost part of the hall, where their meetings transpired. During intermissions, as well as after these conferences, the newcomers were treated to a tour throughout the rest of the medina. Visitors raved about the designers' attention to detail and extolled the delightful idiosyncrasies of the magical medina. Another unidentified chronicler documented the "columns and domes of crystal," as well as the "walls made of falling water." A Moorish author from a neighboring city who claimed to have visited the medina wrote that it took no less than 12,000 loaves of bread to feed the fish in the gardens' ponds each day.

Prior to these meetings, the visitors were ushered to the caliph's throne room, where the pageantry would reach its pinnacle. Paul Cannon, a contributor to *The Visigoth*, described what those visitors saw in a 2016 article entitled "Medina Azahara: Excavation or Building Site?": "From the Caliph's turban would have fallen locks of dyed-black hair (dyed, as after generations of Galicians, Asturians, Castilians, and Franks in their harems...)...[ar-Rahman III] would be richly ornamented and attired in an elegant *almaleque* [a type of luxurious robe], and seated on a throne laden with [quilted] cushions. [Surrounding him] would be Germanic slaves, many of them Franks. Rahman III was wary of his Arab subjects, and preferred to trust mercenaries from outside his society."

What is now a garden in the front of the Salon Rico was once a vast patio with floors made of pristine white and pink marble. The surface of these immaculate floors were routinely buffed and polished so as to achieve the glossiest texture possible. The smoothness and shine of the floors were meant to emulate the pool of water in the story of the Queen of Sheba's first visit to the Israeli king and heir of David, King Solomon.

The true origins of this queen continue to be contested, but the general consensus places her home somewhere in the neighborhood of the Red Sea. More intriguing yet, this mysterious figure is depicted and rebranded in numerous holy books, including the Bible, the Qu'ran, the Aramic *Targum Sheni*, and the Ethiopian *Kebra Negast.* Consequently, the exact details of the meeting between the queen and King Solomon have been distorted by the various renditions of the same tale. In some versions, the queen is conned into engaging in a night of carnal passion with Solomon, eventually bearing for him a son. Other chroniclers deny the existence of such a child and insisted that the queen had been aware of the king's impending advances all along, and that she deliberately "repulsed" him with her unshaven legs and disfigured feet. In the Christian take of the tale, the queen was no more than a messenger of God, "with a very great retinue, with camels bearing spices and very much gold and precious stones." (I Kings 10:2).

In the Qu'ran, Solomon is referred to as Suleiman, and the queen is identified as a sovereign named "Bilqis." As the story goes, one day, Solomon, a blessed monarch gifted with the ability to communicate with animals and spiritual beings known as "*jinn*," was visited by one of his avian spies. The hoopoe bird, a fascinating, scrawny creature with black-and-white striped wings and a crown of bright orange feathers on its head, was a cheerful sight, but the message it bore was not. "I found a woman ruling over them and she has been given of everything and she possesses a mighty throne," the bird proclaimed. Bilqis's subjects were filthy infidels, pagans who knelt before the sun. While the people of Sheba had a powerful kingdom, they "[were] not guided, so that they prostrate not themselves to God." (Sura 27:25).

Concluding that it was his mission to guide Queen Bilqis to the one true path of enlightenment, Solomon invited her to his kingdom. The queen made her apprehension no secret, but with some persistence on the king's part, she finally agreed. Indeed, Solomon had secured her consent, but there remained one problem: he knew that it would take a miracle of some sort to persuade the strong-willed matriarch to denounce her pagan faith. Recalling the bird's mention of the queen's treasured "mighty throne," he hatched a cunning plan to steal her throne and transport it to his palace before her arrival. And that his minions did; they placed Bilqis' bejeweled throne in his "crystal pavilion," the very same the medina's was modeled after, which they then concealed with a scarlet silk cloth.

The queen, arriving the following morning, was steered by Solomon's courtiers to the crystal pavilion. The sensational sight of the glistering crystal and glass walls and the impeccable floors nearly knocked the wind out of Bilqis. She lifted a trembling leg, lingering tentatively in the threshold of the entrance as she peered down at the flawless floor, said to have been so masterfully polished that she mistook it as a wet surface. In doing so, she revealed a set of dainty feet, which greatly surprised Suleiman, for he had been expecting a set of "cloven hooves"; she was, after all, a proponent of a vile faith. The presentation of her throne moments later was enough to open her eyes to the glory of Allah. Bilqis threw herself to her knees, and laid her forehead to the ground. "My Lord, [Allah]," she cried. "Indeed I have wronged myself, and I surrender with Suleiman to God, the Lord of all Being" (Sura 27:45).

In spite of all that ar-Rahman III had accomplished, in the year 961, the bedridden caliph, just a few short breaths away from the cold grips of death, admitted that he was not content. Not even the medina, it seemed, could save him from such a revelation. "I have now reigned above 50 years in victory or peace; beloved by my subjects, dreaded by my enemies, and respected by my allies," ar-Rahman III said. "Riches and honors, power and pleasure, have waited on my call, nor does any earthly blessing appear to have been wanting to my felicity...I have diligently numbered the days of pure and genuine happiness which have fallen to my lot: they amount to 14. O man, Place not thy confidence in this present world!"

While ar-Rahman III is most commonly credited with the creation of the medina, and rightly so, it was reportedly his heir, Al-Hakam II, who was responsible for fleshing out and completing the fantastic palace-city. Al-Hakam II went above and beyond in fulfilling his father's original vision to its utmost potential; others say it was his way of preserving his father's powerful legacy, refusing to allow ar-Rahman III's herculean efforts to go to waste.

When Al-Hakam II, nicknamed "Al-Mustansir Bi-llah," or "He Who Seeks the Victorious Help of Allah," inherited the medina, a contemporary document spelled out which parts were completed: "This year [961 CE] as...[backed by] the Treasury Coffers...We have finished the throne room. Now the whole complex is as immense and complex as Samarra, the Paacio of the Abásidas. And now it's up to [ar-Rahman III and his heir] to compensate the master stonemasons, the weaving workshops, the goldsmiths, and the broncists [sic] who are forging the new fountains of the Medina Azahara..."

Like his father, Al-Hakam II lived for theatricality and grand, ceremonial displays. During regular receptions, the caliphate heir was seated upon fresh quilted cushions with gold pillowcases in his ornate, silk-lined throne. Forming a semi-circle around the throne, placed in the center of the room, were members of Al-Hakam II's retinue, as well as his servants, according to their ranks; advisers and courtiers were closest to the throne, followed by high-ranking generals and officials, soldiers, and servants. Once the doors of the reception hall opened, those in the room, excluding the caliph, rose to their feet, aligning themselves with the visitor's pace.

Before they got down to brass tacks, it was protocol for the visitors to endure a lengthy period of verbose speeches and excessively syrupy poems and compositions that glorified the prideful caliph, leaving visiting ambassadors to "do nothing but feel small before such magnificence." Such examples include this exaltation from an unnamed poet: "You, [my dear Caliph], came to the world with such a good star, that with you, progress makes you forget a year for the next..."

Excessive pageantry aside, the Medina Azahara became more than just a florid, pretentious landmark, because by the time Al-Hakam II was done, it was a fully functioning city. Visitors could find boutiques, restaurants, bakeries, markets (or "*suq*"), inns (*funduq*), public baths (*hammam*), bookshops, libraries, schools, learning centers, workshops, weapons factories, the royal barracks, cavalry housing, and even the Royal Mint.

A coin minted in Medina Azahara 959 or 960 depicting ar-Rahman III

The expansion of the Medina Azahara's libraries is considered by many to be Al-Hakam II's most significant contribution to the palace-city. Ar-Rahman III, often characterized as a bibliophile, stocked the medina's libraries with close to 400,000 religious texts and classical works from around the globe, and during his son's reign, that number swelled to a whopping 600,000, "as many books as all of Christian Europe combined." The medina's royal library was, as a result, the largest of its kind in the world. Al-Hakam II requested that his ambassadors and delegates, as well as visitors from foreign cities, bring him rare manuscripts, rather than trinkets, as gifts.

According to the 13th century historian Ibn Sa'id al-Maghribi, Al-Hakam II's decision to maintain these libraries was also partially motivated by the social politics of the era: "Cordoba [mainly in the Medina Azahara] held more books than any other city in the Al-Andalus, and its inhabitants were the most enthusiastic in caring for its libraries; such collections were regarded as symbols of status and social leadership. Men who had no knowledge whatsoever would make it their business to have a library in their homes...so that they might boast of possessing a *unica*, or copies in the handwriting of a particular calligrapher."

The quantity of Al-Hakam II's libraries was not his only innovation in the field. Knowledge and progress in the Christian hemisphere was stagnant, for their scribes spent the bulk of their time churning out replicas of antique books and archaic religious texts. The scribes employed at the medina, on the other hand, were tasked with not only copying manuscripts, but authoring new books that introduced to the continent Hindu-Arabic numerals, advanced forms of Arabic mathematics, previously unexplored branches of philosophy, and a bevy of groundbreaking medical procedures.

The new caliph further honored his father's memory by erecting 27 free schools for the destitute in Cordoba. He also established a number of academies and learning centers for the middle and upper classes, and improved upon the curriculum of the University of Cordoba. He appointed his brother, Mundhir, general supervisor of education, and staffed the institution with the most sought-after professors and scholars from Baghdad.

Cordoba was, as the chronicler Imamuddin put it, "the same to Europe as the head to the body...Al-Hakam II raised the civilization in [Hispania] to such a height that Cordoba served as a beacon in the darkness which then prevailed in Europe." And the beating heart of this intellectual powerhouse of a city was the Medina Azahara.

All that Glitters is Not Gold

"And walk not on the earth with conceit and arrogance. Verily, you can neither rend nor penetrate the earth, nor can you attain a stature like the mountains height..." – Al-Isra 17:37

Exactly how many residents inhabited the Medina Azahara is unknown, but historians estimate that there were at least 13,000 officials of varying ranks, coupled with more than 4,000 slaves and pages scattered throughout the middle and lowest tiers of the palace-city. In a fruitful effort to attract even more residents to the medina, Al-Hakam II offered 400 dirhams a piece to the subjects who relocated to the premises with their families. The diligence and tenacity he injected into the guardianship of the medina's libraries also rewarded the caliph with an influx of intellectuals, who applied for residency within the medina on their own volition.

Such tempting rumors included the description provided by a eunuch named Talid, who also served as the chief librarian of the medina's principal library: "The bookcases were made of polished and perfumed wood. Golden inscriptions indicated the contents of the shelves and several rooms in the palace were set apart for work of copying, illuminating, gilding, and binding books for which the most skillful persons of both sexes were employed..."

Cordoba, particularly its Shining City, shot to fame as Europe's premier book market, one wherein "the literary productions of every country were available for sale." The city's surplus of flax, which allowed for "cheap, flax-based paper," only maximized its profits, and the equal opportunities provided to both genders and people of all faiths and backgrounds made the medina even more appealing to those in the central capital, as well as its neighboring cities. Entrepreneurs and working class laborers flocked to the palace-city, drawn not only to the variegated workshops, factories, and business units available, but the prospects of profit, further developing their skills, and working alongside the most talented individuals in all of Moorish Spain.

When the Moors first captured Hispania, they brought with them a miscellany of scientific knowledge and innovative technologies, one of which was a copper still they called the "*alambique*." Christian Spaniards greatly benefited from these copper stills, which they used for the production and distillation of wine. As the Muslim Spaniards were prohibited from consuming alcohol, as per the laws of the Qu'ran, the stills in the medina were used only for the manufacturing of medicines and various perfumes.

A large number of the medina's workshops were devoted to leather working, as the Moors were famed for their mastery of fine leather working. The trademark "*qurtuban*" or "*cordovan*" leather fabricated by the medina's workshops are said to have been of the highest quality in Europe, and as a result, pungent, sleek strips of leather were frequently used by the royals and nobles during special celebrations. Al-Hakam II, for instance, removed the silky linen tablecloths that usually graced his banquet tables prior to the visits of foreign dignitaries, replacing them instead with fine leather table runners. The contrast provided by the dark and russet undercurrents of the leather, the caliph believed, added an extra sparkle to the golden goblets, crystal glasses, and silver dishware laid out on the tables.

The medina's markets, otherwise known as bazaars, were located in the lowermost tier, a particularly exuberant section of the compound. The casual chatter and the jingles rattled out by vendors, married with the mingled scents of the flavorful and fragrant spices, and the colorful sight of the markets' selection of fruits, vegetables, meat, ceramics, Arabic silks, and other commodities, made the area a sight to behold. The palace-city's winding streets and alleyways were congested with dozens of stalls, each cramped space equipped with a "red-ochre colored door...tilted upwards to open (not unlike a garage door)." The door, when raised, acted as an awning that shielded the silks, ceramics, and other precious goods from the rain.

If possible, the patios that punctuated the complex were just as lively. Jesús Atalaya, a participant of a recent "patio competition," noted the importance of patio life in the days of Moorish Spain: "The patio was, and in many cases still is, the center, the heart and the soul of the houses in the old part of Cordoba. They were also the heart of the family, where people would spend their time together, eating and socializing."

Yet another constantly bustling part of the medina was its network of *hammam*, or public baths. It functioned as a social hub and promoted sanitation, but it was, at the same time, a sacred facility the locals regarded as of utmost importance, secondary to the mosque. Followers of the faith dutifully entered these baths or dipped into the medina's ablution wells, thoroughly cleansing themselves with water – to them a symbol of purity – in preparation for formal prayers, a ritual known as "*wudu*."

With all of that said, who have chosen to romanticize the Medina Azahara and the allegedly harmonious coexistence of Spaniard Muslims, Jews, and Christians often turn a blind eye to the bleaker, more sobering realities of life in the palace-city, as well as throughout the Al-Andalus. This passage, penned by the *Secular African Society* in August of 2013, shines a light on the grim actualities the slaves and the eunuchs of the medina were made to face: "The Islamic slave trade, which was extensively more atrocious than the Atlantic slave trade...affected a wider demography of indigenous peoples, and went on longer...The unprecedented pan-continental economic success of raiding infidel communities and enslaving war captives was exclusive to Islamic culture...Naturally, it gave way to the demand for eunuchs." Eunuchs, the society explains, "were the preferred male slave choice for consumers, because they posed lesser security risks at the harems, in the palace, and in the domestic affairs of ordinary Muslims."

The slaves and eunuchs in the medina, like those throughout the Islamic Empire, were mainly raid hostages and war captives from Persia, as well as other parts of Europe, Africa, and the Indian subcontinent. It was not unheard of for Muslim nobles to castrate their slaves, a practice that was controversial even for the time, as the Qu'ran denounced all forms of body mutilation for any reason. As a matter of fact, a *hadith* stated that a man who castrates a slave shall himself receive the blade. As such, a loophole most used was to purchase slaves that had already undergone castration.

Most of the eunuchs that lived in the palace-city were employed as bodyguards for the harem. A pair of eunuchs would be posted outside the doors of the concubines' residences, and a larger group was stationed outside the private homes of the caliph's favorite concubines. Due to the drastic reduction of the castrated men's sexual impulses and desires, only they were entrusted with keeping the caliph's concubines "unsullied." Both ar-Rahman III and Al-Hakam II apparently afforded the eunuchs of their courts with the same respect they gave to notable officials, and even awarded a few of them with more important, salaried positions.

On a brighter note, the community and culture developed within the Medina Azahara is believed to have been essential in thrusting the Al-Andalus into the next phase of its golden age. The treasures that ar-Rahman III hoarded within the medina's walls were far from just material goods, because he also transformed the palace-city into the headquarters of Moorish Spain's most celebrated artists, musicians, authors, poets, scientists, mathematicians, astronomers, botanists, and medical practitioners. One alleged resident of the Medina Azahara was the mathematician named Ibn Mu'adh al-Jayyani, who authored the first-ever treatise on spherical trigonometry and various commentaries on important classical works, such as Euclid's *Elements*. Another was Maslamah al-Majriti, now recognized as the "first original mathematician and astronomer of the Al-Andalus." A frequent visitor of the palace-city was the theologian, jurist, and professor of medicine, Ibn Hazm, remembered for the advances he made in hygiene and medical ethics. It was Hazm who urged doctors to not only practice patience, benevolence, and understanding, but to also keep their hair and nails short and trimmed at all times.

Sadly, time had a far more rapid and adverse impact on the medina than even ar-Rahman III had anticipated on his deathbed. Historians today say that it was Al-Hakam II's abrupt death by stroke in October of 976 that triggered the inevitable fall of the palace-city. Upon the 61-year-old Al-Hakam II's death, the caliphate was inherited by his 11-year-old son, Hisham II al-Mu'ayad. On account of Hisham's age, the Prime Minister of Cordoba, Al-Mansur, was appointed his regent.

Al-Mansur took full advantage of the unique opportunity he had been presented with, rearranging the power structure and layout of the city as he pleased. By the year 981, the regent had succeeded in relocating the entire court, the royal mint, the army (and barracks), and numerous other government buildings to central Cordoba. The Medina Azahara, quite literally a hollow shell of what it once was, slipped into a rapid decline.

Due to what little was left of the soldiers in the medina, the palace-city's defenses were dramatically weakened. The sudden and visible loss of the medina's once untouchable status gradually drove away the wealthy, as well as the intellectuals, artisans, merchants, and business owners that once made this emporium of talents so distinguished, and further repelled potential inhabitants.

What permanently doomed the medina occurred during a civil war sometime between the years of 1010 and 1013. These assailants, described as "North African Islamic purists" who despised what they deemed the overly liberal character of the palace-city, laid siege to the Medina Azahara, sending the last of its residents fleeing for good. The marauders toppled over monument after monument, defaced the compound's most prominent buildings, and robbed the medina of its treasures before torching the palace-city to the ground.

For close to a thousand years, the Medina Azahara festered and rotted away, forgotten by the descendants of those who once praised the palace-city. In the first few centuries that followed, architects and scavengers salvaged what they could from the medina's ruins, utilizing these historical components in brand new structures. Some of the fallen marble pillars from the caliph's palace, for example, were reused for the roofs of common Cordoban houses. Ashlar blocks used in the walls, foundations, and facades of the medina's old buildings can now be seen in centuries-old cow sheds. A few of the artifacts allegedly rescued from the rubble are also housed in museums and royal residences in the cities of Malaga and Granada.

The city became such an obscure fragment of the past that it was left out of maps for centuries on end. Following the Christian "reconquest" of Moorish Spain, locals simply saw the ruins as no more than an unmarked section of a place they called "Old Cordova." Many would most likely shrug and mistake it for an old Roman city.

It was only towards the end of the 1800s that the city's memory of the Medina Azahara was restored. This was thanks to a publicized, then popularized Spanish translation of an ancient book written in Arabic, which made several references to a glorious "Shining City" that once lay just a few kilometers away. Still, the ruins of the medina remained untouched until the 1911 excavation headed by a local architect named Riocardo Velazques Bosco.

12 years later, the Medina Azahara was crowned a "national monument." An architect with a similarly glowing portfolio named Felix Hernandez replaced Bosco upon his death in late 1923, that same year. Hernandez continued the first phase of the excavations, which were centered on "discovering the general structure" and determining the rough shape of the medina's layout. In 1944, Hernandez went on to launch the next phase of the excavations, which spotlighted the most central part of the caliph's palace, which he estimated to be at least 10.5 hectares in size. Sometime between the late months of 1944 and the early months of 1945, Hernandez's men uncovered the Salon Rico, and they subsequently proceeded to carry out a general remodeling of the reception hall throughout the 1950s.

In 1964, local headlines reported the archaeologists' unveiling of the Mezquita Aljama, and in the following year, the discovery of the central "crystal pavilion" of the Salon Rico. 20 years later, the ruins of the medina were branded a dependency of the Regional Government of Andalusia. From that point forward, the governing body aided in the direction and financing of excavations, as well as studies on the origins and history of the brilliant palace-city, paying special attention to its defenses and the royal fortress.

Towards the end of the 20th century, campaigns aiming to educate the public about the historical significance of the Medina Azahara took the nation by storm, and in the early years of the 21st century, the ruins of the medina's Casa de Jafar became available for public viewing. In 2007, a second, smaller mosque was discovered in the lowermost level of the palace-city, located by the west wall. It's believed this was where blacksmiths, merchants, mint staff, and other commoners worshiped.

Today, only about 10% of the medina's ruins have been excavated and restored, which means scholars and everyone interested in the site still have to take the existing descriptions of the palace-city with a hefty grain of salt. Only in July of 2018 did the Medina Azahara earn a coveted spot on the UNESCO World Heritage List, an honor that its enthusiasts say is long overdue. A much more extensive series of renovations on the Salon Rico, as announced by the Minister of Culture, Miguel Angel Vaquez, is due to take place in the last quarter of 2018, an ambitious endeavor that will cost authorities an astounding €500 million.

The Final Moorish Expansions

"Your arches, your terraces,

Shimmer with the light

That once flashed in the valley of Aiman,

Your soaring minaret all aglow

In the resplendence of Gabriel's glory..." - Allama Muhammad Iqbal, "The Mosque of Cordoba" (1933)

Following the fatal stroke suffered by al-Hakam II in mid-October of 976, his 11-year-old son, Hisham II, was declared the new caliph of Córdoba. Given the child's age and obvious inexperience, his queen mother, Subh, and the royal chamberlain Al-Mansur Ibn Abi Aamir (also known as "Almanzor") were appointed as his regents. By 981, however, the latter had managed to do away with the young caliph's brother, along with anyone else that posed a threat, and succeeded in securing the throne for himself and ruling over Córdoba as its de facto caliph until 1002.

In 987, about 6 years into his reign, al-Mansur launched the last and most significant phase of the Mezquita's Moorish expansions. As ambitious as his plans were, the multiple remodeling projects, internal power struggles, and the often unnecessary and extravagant purchases made by previous caliphs had taken a visible toll on the royal treasury. This is reflected in the tools and materials used for the expansion in question, described as cheap and inferior in contrast to those used in former expansions.

Taking into account the lack of free room to the south of the mosque, for the structure was now closer than ever to the Guadalquivir, Al-Mansur instructed the architects to extend the Mezquita to the east with 8 new naves. To create the space for these new naves, the self-proclaimed caliph forcibly commandeered the civilian houses that stood in the path of the augmentation; whether or not the homeowners were compensated for the unexpected relocation is unclear.

Unable to afford the onyx, jasper, marble, and granite used in the columns during previous renovations, al-Mansur's architects had to make do with the hunks of limestone they were provided. The wedges that made up the curve of the arches, now made of monotone stone and brick, had to be manually painted red to match the older arches. The tight budget also prevented them from demolishing, moving, and reconstructing the prayer niche and maqsura. As such, these features were no longer centered by the qibla wall.

Additionally, al-Mansur broadened the courtyard and added to the mosque an underground cistern (or "jabiya") attached to a water channel that led to the sahn from the northeastern corner.

By the time the final stages of the Moorish expansion came to a close, the Mezquita had almost doubled in size. The mosque was now over 40,000 square feet, capable of hosting up to 40,000 at one time and possibly the biggest mosque in the world. Its lengthy arcades and hypnotically uniform rows of striped arches added to the illusion of the mosque's perpetuity. More importantly, the Mezquita, the Umayyad dynasty's greatest showpiece, became not only the central hub for Moorish worshipers in Western Europe, but a breeding ground for Al-Andalusian scholars and intellectuals, who gathered here to study and exchange ideas about literature, arts, and sciences.

At first glance, the exterior of the Mezquita seems underwhelming compared to the interior. An aerial view of the mosque shows an enormous, but rather drab rectangular complex. The verdant courtyard made up roughly 25% of the premises; columns of skinny gabled roofs stretched from one wall to the other, all in the same sandy-brown hue consistent with its neighboring buildings and structures.

This excerpt, penned by James C. Murphy, contributor to *Islamic Arts & Architecture*, further expands on the technical details of the Mezquita's facade: "The [Mezquita] is of a quadrangular form, 620-ft in length from north to south, and 440-ft in breadth from east to west; it was originally surrounded by 4 streets, which were designed to prevent any other building from coming in contact with it. Of the 21 doors, which it is said to have originally had, 5 only are now remaining... Of the 620-ft, which compose the length of the mosque, 210 were appropriated to the north side, to the formation of a court, communicating by means of a gate of modern erection, and known by the appellation of the Gait of Pardon..."

That being said, the dull exterior of the mosque is now believed to have been a conscious decision, one made with the welfare of the mosque's internal treasures in mind. The walls that girdled this massive compound were among the sturdiest in this region, and they were topped with crenellated battlements and buttresses designed to emulate fortress walls and stave off any potential intruders. The "alternating headers and stretchers" in the outer walls, as termed by Marvin Mills in his book, *The Origin of the Mosque of Córdoba: Secrets of Andalusia*, was a style the Moors borrowed from Roman architects.

These walls, particularly the section in the southwestern corner of the establishment, have naturally begun to show signs of wear. Some parts of the original smoky-gray plaster have deteriorated, revealing the bones of the internal stonework. Conversely, the handsome doors interspersed between the piers and buttresses, adorned with stucco fretwork laced with earth-made mosaics, have managed to withstand exposure to the elements for the last 1,200 years.

Américo Toledano's picture of the Puerta de los Deanes

Américo Toledano's picture of the Puerta de San Ildefonso

Jose Luis Filpo's picture of the Puerta de San Esteban

It was around this time that the sahn by the main entrance received its current name for the first time: the Patio de los Naranjos, or Courtyard of Oranges. Christian sources, however, assert that it was not the Moors, but 16th century bishop Francisco Reinos who first introduced oranges into the Mezquita courtyard. As suggested by its name, the patio was brightened up by rows upon rows of fragrant orange, pomegranate, lemon, and an assortment of other trees bearing exotic fruit, many of which were imported from Damascus. Joining the already diverse array of fruit trees in the courtyard were palm trees planted in the 13th century, as well as cypress and olive trees added to the collection sometime in the 18th century. Today, only 98 of the 18th century orange trees remain.

When the Mezquita was first constructed, Emir ar-Rahman I installed a simple hydraulics system that would replenish the ablution fountains and water the plants in the sahn. 20 years before Al-Mansur's expansion of the mosque, al-Hakam II amplified the water supply by adding to it a water channel, cocooned in lead piping, that connected the mosque to the mountains northwest of the city limits. A visitor to the mosque once marveled at how water "flowed into the mosque's irrigation canals and ablution basins on the east and west sides," indicating that another ablution well had been planted to meet the needs of the Mezquita's growing patrons.

The following passage illustrates how the mosque's irrigation system worked: "Water was collected first by a simple catchment system that collected and funneled [rainwater] from the roof gables into the courtyard, unseen from the ground. During the dry season, water was also brought by aqueduct that was an extension of a Roman aqueduct network, repaired in the Umayyad period. Through its intelligent harvesting of water, the mosque was linked to the larger environment of mountains, plain, river, and city."

The patio itself was a multi-purpose facility; in addition to being a space for ritualistic cleansing and meditation, one could also attend riveting lectures and even religious trials hosted by Muslim elders.

Needless to say, the interior of the finished mosque was every bit as spellbinding as its exterior was lusterless. 19 aisles made up the prayer hall – measuring about 350 feet in length and 14 feet in width apiece – oriented north to south, and slightly narrower and shorter aisles can be found arranged from the east to west of the mosque. These aisles were segregated by the beautiful horseshoe arches and close-to-identical columns, each pillar (made of either "verd antique" or "red marble veined with white") about 9 feet tall and 18 inches in diameter. The capitals of these pillars, with the exception of those erected during al-Mansur's time, were sculpted out of white marble flecked with gold. These columns, as well as the garnishes on the roof, bear a striking resemblance to those in the Alhambra.

The timber used in the mosque's ornate woodwork is a feature very much admired by many modern architects today. The majority of the wood used was derived from the alerce, or "Fitzroya" tree, a breed of the cypress family also commonly linked to cedar and white larch (pine). Fortunately, the Guadalquivir-adjacent forests of medieval Córdoba and neighboring cities had plenty of these famously "incorruptible" alerce trees. Like the water canals constructed by al-Hakam II, the woodwork on the roof and facade was encased in lead for extra protection against age and weather.

The prayer niche, rebuilt and glamorized by al-Hakam II and slightly enhanced by Al-Mansur, was regarded by its architects and worshipers as the most stunning part of the Mezquita. The main door, or portal leading to the mihrab, consisted of a large horseshoe arch, framed by a rectangular panel, or an "alfiz," embossed in gold. The mosaic-coated wedges of the arch, which came in shades of blacks, reds, golds, and whites, were created by a mosaic artist hand-selected by Byzantine Emperor Nicephoras II Phocas. The Moorish caliphs requested that the mosaic artist be knowledgeable in Umayyad architectural design, and that he incorporate the Islamic swirls, floral, and vegetal motifs found in the Great Mosque of Damascus. On top of sending over a master mosaic artist, Emperor Nicephoras also sent along about 3,527 pounds of gold mosaic cubes.

The ivory-white "scallop-shell" dome of the prayer niche served as a natural loudspeaker of sorts for the imam (the elder leading the services), projecting his voice throughout the Mezquita. The Kufic lettering engraved along the midnight-blue strips of marble bordering the alfiz on all three sides, as well as the red bands between the small black marble pillars and the base of the arch, refer to more verses from the Quran, and listed the names of the caliph, architects, and crew members behind the building and renovations. Al-Hakam II, for instance, is identified as the "instrument through which the structure was built and completed." The institution and indisputability of his kingdom was also declared in the inscriptions, abolishing "what came before it, and...[proclaiming] the ascendancy of a new world order and the establishment of God's caliphate on earth."

By the end of al-Mansur's expansion, the interior of the prayer hall had been split up into four sections. These wings were delineated by two rows of "clustered pillars" that intersected at right angles. Three of these wings were made accessible to the public, including women and children, and the last, which lay in the south-east corner of the mosque, was restricted to the caliph, imams, and other high-ranking Muslim priests. It was this exclusive section of the Mezquita – or as it was known to the worshipers, the Zancarron, or "Sanctuary" – that housed the mosque's principal Quran and other religious apparatus.

The strategic placement of the Mezquita in the 10th century – the prepossessing complex was a prominent landmark on the so-called Route of the Caliphate – made it even more accessible to locals, as well as pilgrims and merchants traveling along the well-trodden path. Simply put, this trail served as a bridge for the Caliph and Nasrid capitals, connecting the most important cities in Islamic Spain, including Córdoba, Granada, and the settlements in Jaén. Apart from merchants, art and literary connoisseurs from faraway lands also made the long trek to witness the incomparable beauty and the electrifying learning environment within the courtyard of the Mezquita firsthand. Many of these foreign worshipers, scholars, and visitors brought home with them ideas – architectural and otherwise – that they eventually wove into their own cultures. The general grandeur of the city during this time is best encapsulated in the words of Charles Emmanuel Dufourq: "Never before, neither Rome nor Paris, the most populated cities of the western Christian medieval, got anywhere near the splendor of Córdoba, the largest urban nucleus in medieval Europe..."

At the same time, the placement of the Mezquita made it a flashpoint for the tensions brewing between the Christians and Muslims in the Iberian Peninsula. Many today already question the veracity of the "interfaith utopia" the Moorish rulers of Spain allegedly promoted, but either way, the latter caliphs of the city were evidently far less tolerant than their predecessors. Under the reign of al-Mansur, for example, the status of Christians and Jews as "dhimmis," or second-class citizens, was further reinforced. Aside from the crippling increase in taxes and duties that Spanish Arabs and Muslims were exempt from, the caliph ordered numerous raids that targeted Christian and Jewish churches and synagogues. The grand Santiago de Compostela was one of the Christian establishments that al-Mansur demanded be torched to the ground, and the worshipers were then shackled and made to march to the capital with their dismantled church bells on their backs.

The non-Muslims of Spain became further incensed by the often petty restrictions imposed on them that were decreed by the later caliphs and preserved by the Almoravids and Almohads who succeeded them after the collapse of the caliphate in 1031. For one, Christians and Jews were prohibited from dwelling in houses that surpassed their Muslim neighbors' in height. They were never to display any signs of their faith outside of their homes, and they were prohibited from conducting Masses in public spaces. In fact, the mere act of carrying a Bible in one's pocket was grounds for arrest, and sometimes even murder. Moreover, Christians and Jews were banned from putting to work Muslim servants, and forced to clear the path whenever they saw a Muslim heading in their direction. The senseless massacres and unjust persecutions only exacerbated the boiling bad blood between the Muslims and non-Muslims.

It would only be a matter of time before the Christians would attempt to reclaim the land, leading to the Mezquita's most dramatic makeover yet.

The Return of the Christians

"Christ redeemed us on the hard arms of the Cross, and His knight will not serve Him in any other way." – attributed to Saint Ferdinand III of Castile

In the wake of the messy and convoluted power struggle between the warring taifa states, the Córdoban treasury was wobbling on its last leg, and the morale of the public was progressively declining, for it was they who suffered the worst of the lethargic economy and the concurrent deceleration in the development of science, technology, and culture. By the early decades of the 13th century, the Almohad rulers, embroiled in a violent civil war, were struggling to keep up the guise of unity, but it was too late. Those outside the city fringes had already tuned in to the increasing internal friction of the once unconquerable Córdoba for several years, attentively observing the unfolding events and waiting for the right moment to pounce.

On a frosty and stormy winter's evening in December 1235, an intrepid band of Castilian knights shimmied up to the city's defensive walls and daringly penetrated Córdoba. There, the knights took the initiative and laid siege to one of the smaller suburbs. Delighted by the almost effortless occupation of that suburb, the Castilian general sent one of his soldiers back to Castile to inform King Ferdinand III about their victory, as well as the current fragility of the valuable Moorish territory. Ferdinand, who was more than pleased by the turn of events and doubly impressed by the ambitiousness of the warriors, sent along reinforcements and supplies shortly thereafter.

A contemporary depiction of King Ferdinand III of Castile

By the spring of 1236, the Castilian king activated the culminating phase of his plans for the capture of Córdoba and mobilized his troops. According to the chroniclers of his life, the king himself, mounted atop a mighty white stallion, charged into the city, riding front and center. Together with his men, Ferdinand seized the city's principal castle, set fire to numerous Muslim public structures, spaces, and fields, and relentlessly harassed the occupants until what was left of the city surrendered in June.

In the weeks that followed, the Castilian king administered to his Muslim prisoners a taste of the medicine that the Moors' Christian captives had previously suffered. Christian and Jewish villagers lined the streets, whispering and watching in frenzied awe as the frail and spent prisoners lugged the old bells of the Santiago de Compostela, strapped to their backs with rusty chains, back to where they came from.

The Castilian king's first order of business was to rebrand the mosque as a Christian worshiping place. On the 29th of June, 1236, the new subjects of the Castilian crown congregated at the former mosque and witnessed the first dedication of the Mezquita to the Virgin Mary, marked by "rituals of purification." Though where exactly the consecration was held is unclear, Christian worshipers began to pray towards the mihrab in the east (which contained the host and main Bible of the parish), rather than the south of the former mosque.

Thenceforth, the church, later reclassified as a cathedral, was to be known as the "Catedral de Nuestra Señora de la Asunción," or in English, the "Cathedral of Our Lady of the Assumption." For the next 250 years, Christian services and gatherings were confined to the newest wing attached by al-Hakam II, likely because that section most closely echoed the features of a traditional Christian church.

Despite the name change, the Mezquita, as the Moors knew it, remained relatively unchanged, save for the addition of a few small chapels. A few weeks after the dedication ceremony, King Ferdinand approved the construction of the Mezquita's first cathedral choir in the nave facing the prayer niche, as well as a simple, but elegant altar assembled for Saint Peter.

In 1257, Ferdinand's son and successor, Alfonso X, added to the Christian-occupied vestibule the Capilla Mayor, or "Royal Chapel," which came with an altar directed towards the east of the mosque-turned-cathedral. This undertaking, however, would only be completed during the latter half of the 14th century, as indicated by the writing on the skirting board: "This is the high king Enrique (Enrique II). Honoring the body of the king, his father, he commanded this chapel to be built. It was finished in the year 1371."

A contemporary portrait of Alfonso X

Michael Clarke's picture of the Capilla Mayor

    This square chapel was built atop the arches erected by al-Hakam II, and people could only enter the chapel through the staircase of the Chapel of Villaviciosa, which was connected to the western wall of the Capilla Mayor. The mudejar art, a fusion of Christian and Islamic aesthetics, are especially remarkable, and a passage from an Artencordoba article describes the chapel in further detail: "A beautiful tiling skirting board, with geometric decoration based on laces, rhombuses, and crestings, went along the perimeter of the chapel, and over it the decoration of the 4 walls started. Along the eastern wall, there is an original plaster frieze with heraldic motifs of Castila y Leon, epigraphic Arabic decoration, and small lobed arches. From the same frieze, 5 polylobed arches start, displayed irregularly, from which a decoration is developed based on rhombuses over an Arabesque ackground...On the western wall...there is a wide horseshoe arch, inside which there were originally the 2 alcoves entering the chapel."

Finally, displayed in the nook of the altar was a large, full-color sculpture carved in the likeness of the king-turned-saint Ferdinand III of Castile. The conqueror of Córdoba, seen with a pencil-thin mustache and rich caramel-brown ringlets, wore a dazzling gilded crown and a red-and-gold cape draped over his royal tunic, lined with white, ornamented felt. On one hand, he balanced what appears to be a globe, and in the other, he brandished his rapier.

An unnamed monk who visited the mosque-cathedral during this time wrote these glowing words about the marvelous structure: "[The Mezquita was] a temple worthy of all manner of praise, whose spectacular beauty reanimates the spirit of whoever contemplates it. It is the glory of Spain and distinctive symbol of the honor of Córdoba, illustrious seat of its Bishop; a monument that honors the kings who exacted such injurious revenge, a revenge that makes us shed tears for its ancient owners...The talent of the architects determined an extreme structural clarity, so that wherever one looks, his gaze marches on majestically...What can we say of this famous temple? The historians refer to the prodigious attributes of only 7 buildings in the world...But who will appreciate in the future these monuments as superior to others, when contemplating such a temple in our city?"

Up until the Reconquista era in the late 1400s, the mosque-cathedral remained more or less under the sole jurisdiction of the Córdoban royals, but not long after the Christians' capture of the last Moorish footholds in and Granada in January 1492, the reins were transferred to the hands of the Catholic Church.

A few months before the fateful fall of Granada, the Córdoban bishop, Iñigo Manrique de Lara, presented his plans to recast the mosque as a proper cathedral, one that would officially usher in the Christian chapter of the Mezquita. Bishop Iñigo's sketches were supposedly so irreversibly transformative that the Catholic queen consort, Isabella I of Castile, openly objected to the drastic makeover. Her vocal opposition, along with some added pressure from other critics, was supposedly enough to persuade the bishop to considerably whittle down his alterations.

Isabella

Even so, the vast Gothic-style nave that Iñigo eventually injected into the Mezquita created a tactile disruption among the Moorish, Roman, and Visigothic themes of the original complex. The dome above the quartet of portals in the transept, each gaping archway measuring two stories in height, was almost bland compared to the domes built by Moorish-employed Byzantine architects. The interior of the white-and-gold cupola featured a medallion in its center with vertical strips of Baroque design fanning out like the rays of the sun. That said, the spotless white of the stuccoed walls, vaulted ceilings, and panels above the overlapping red-and-white horseshoe arches of the Gothic space, which ran westward from the altar, was a breathtaking sight to behold. The latticework of gold clinging to the walls, which came in diamond, butterfly, and other geometric patterns, gave the area an extra touch of opulence.

Iñigo also commissioned local goldsmith Enrique de Arfe to construct the Processional Custody of Corpus Christi, also referred to as the "Processional Cross." Now on display in the Mezquita's Cathedral Treasury, the tower-like structure, which appears to be made out of entirely silver to the untrained eye, was composed of four parts. The first was the base, decorated with "trefoil arches and filigree points" and made up of a total of 18 scenes illustrating the 18 scenes of the "Public Life, Passion, and Resurrection of Christ." The minuscule bronze figures in the carvings were only about two inches tall, a testament to the talent and dexterity of de Arfe. The second part of the tower, which consists of the cylindrical "temple of the glass and gold case," was perched upon a scroll-like base seated with angels. The third part of the tower, the "temple of the Assumption," is a cluster of towers constructed by silversmith Bernabe Garcia de los Reyes that star the Virgin Mary and are joined to the rest of the towers with seraphs on the backs of dolphins. Crowning this exquisite masterpiece was the "bell temple," which came with six tiny bells inside the cupola, resting upon a group of hexagonal towers woven together by wreaths of flowers.

By the 16th century, the swiftly burgeoning wealth and power of the Catholic Church in Western Europe had allowed Spanish authorities to destroy even more mosques and replace them with palatial cathedrals. Bishop Alonso Manrique de Lara, the first cousin of Iñigo, refused to let the opportunity for yet another renovation slip through the cracks of his fingers. Thus, Alonso submitted another set of blueprints to the upper levels of the Church, including a plan to refurbish the Villaviciosa Chapel, otherwise known as the "Original Main Chapel." Those from the town council who deemed the Gothic nave an eyesore that muddied perfection launched another rash of protests, and their aggressive petitions eventually reached Holy Roman Emperor Charles V. Once again, church authorities partially acquiesced and curbed the magnitude of Alonso's proposed renovations, but they proceeded with the demolitions in the spring of 1523.

Charles V

The Capilla de Villaviciosa, marked by its pointed transversal arches, was situated under the Lucernario de Villaviciosa, the skylight installed by al-Hakam II. The vaulted ceiling, capped by a wooden gabled roof, was enriched with plant-like motifs on coffers, as well as Latin and Greek epigraphs hailing "Jesus Christ the Savior." The Italian-Byzantine frescoes painted in the chapel back in 1351, showing key biblical scenes starring Christ and numerous saints (the work of artist Alonso Martinez de Toledo), were also polished again. Only two of these frescoes – the Head of Christ and the Head of the Virgin – have survived the test of time, and they are now exhibited at the Museum of Fine Arts in Córdoba.

Ingo Mehling's picture of the Capilla de Villaviciosa

Other Christian chapels eventually built within the Mezquita include the following: the Capilla de La Conversion de San Pablo, or the "Chapel of the Conversion of Saint Paul"; the Capilla de San Esteban y San Bartolome, or the "Chapel of Saint Esteban and Saint Bartholomew"; the Capilla de la Natividad de Nuestra Señora, or the "Chapel of the Nativity of Our Lady"; the Capilla de Las Animas del Purgatorio, or the "Chapel of the Souls of Purgatory"; the Capilla de Nestra Señora de la Concepcion, or the "Chapel of Our Lady of Conception"; the Capilla de Santa Teresa, or the "Chapel of Saint Teresa"; and finally, the Capilla de Santa Ines, or the "Chapel of Santa Ines."

Michael Clarke's picture of the Capilla de la Concepcion

It did not take long for buyer's remorse to set in. When Charles V visited the Mezquita in 1526, he was sickened by the painful sight of the rubble strewn across the floor, these priceless and historic works of Moorish art now irreparable. He reportedly mused, "Had I known what this was, I would not have allowed it to reach the ancient part." He then said the now immortal words to the architects and designers responsible for the damage: "Habéis tomado algo único y lo habéis convertido en algo mundano" ("You have built what you or others might have built anywhere, but you have destroyed something that was unique in this world").

The chief architect tasked with executing Bishop Alonso's vision, Hernán Ruiz I, had voiced his qualms regarding the extent of the damage the demolitions would have caused, so he made a conscious effort to retain some of the Moorish charm. To start with, he paved an Arabesque ambulatory, or walkway, around the transept of the mosque-cathedral. He then salvaged the columns, capitals, and stones from the rubble to reuse them in the new Islamic-style arches that he peppered around the ambulatory. Inside of the mosque-cathedral, he pinpointed the bulk of his remodeling to the south of the existing choir, installing his Gothic vaults there. His subtle additions to this wing of the Mezquita can only be detected if one inspected the Baroque detailing on the ribbed vaults up close.

Hernán's son, Hernán Ruiz II, was not as mindful of the former mosque's Moorish elements. Under his direction, laborers hoisted up the walls of the transept, underpinned and supported by eight buttresses. The Gothic ribbed vault over the arms of the transept and the Villaviciosa Chapel were also hammered into place and enhanced with triangular, pastel-toned frescoes featuring scenes from the Assumption of the Virgin Mary, as well as a medley of disciples, cherubs, angels, saints, and an obscure regal figure that is believed by many to be none other than Emperor Charles V. A scroll-like tablet, known as a "cartouche," was also hung up, engraved with a long passage written for the Virgin Mother.

The minaret, casting a shadow over the rest of the structures in the compound at 177 feet, was then the tallest building in all of Córdoba. The Alminar remained mostly untouched – apart from its rebranding as a Christian belfry tower in 1360 – until the 21st of September, 1589, when a terrible storm threatened to topple the tower. A few years later, with the octagonal spire above the clock bell a breath away from disintegrating, the Cathedral Chapter voted to give the tower a much-needed makeover. A temporary campanile containing six bells was placed atop the Door of Forgiveness in the meantime so that local Christians could continue to be summoned to services.

In July 1593, Hernán Ruiz III kicked off the renovations. Assisting him was a select team of experts that included Asensio de Madea, the Senior Master of the Cathedral of Seville, Juan Coronado, and Juan de Ochoa. The upper half of the old Alminar was dismantled, and a fresh tower, complete with a new body of bells, was wrapped around the core of the Moorish tower.

When Hernán Ruiz III died in 1606, Juan Sequero de Matilla inherited the project. He added a large Roman clock below the belfry. Gaspar de la Peña designed the cupola over the bells, which soon sheltered the statue of Saint Raphael, sculpted by Pedro de la Paz and Bernabé Gómez del Río.

Like most Christian bell towers, the bells in the campanile of the Mezquita were given their own names. The names of these bells, which included the "Assumption" and the "Saint Zouilus," were etched into the bottom or the inside of the bells, along with their date of manufacture, the emblems of the architects and the bishop that played a hand in their production.

Ingo Mehling's picture of the bell tower from the Court of Oranges

A little over a century later, the bell tower took another beating during yet another storm in 1727, followed by a devastating earthquake just 28 years later. Not only did these natural disasters take several bites out of the tower's torso, the base of the Saint Raphael was left severely fractured. As such, in 1755, French architect Baltasar Dreveton was employed to repair the tower, a project that took another eight years to complete.

When Córdoba entered the golden age of the Renaissance years, the Mezquita witnessed yet another tide of modifications and additions. Renowned Italian artist Pablo de Céspedes, who held the appellation of "Prebendary of the Cathedral" between 1577 and 1608, painted the four gorgeous pieces on display in the Capilla de Santa Ana - The Last Supper, Elijah Being Comforted By an Angel, The Meeting of Abraham and Melchizedek, and Samson with the Lion. The Last Supper, notable for its cool tones and the emotive nuances of the figures' expressions, was the centerpiece for the altar. It was later enshrined in an ornate gilded frame chiseled by Juan de Ortuño.

Italian Mannerist painter César Arbasia, endorsed by de Céspedes, joined the crew soon thereafter. In 1583, he was sent to work in the Parroquia del Sagrario, which, until then, was home to the Chapter Library and the Chapel of Santiago. The Parroquia was at this stage en route to becoming the principal sanctuary of the cathedral. Under the watchful eye of Bishop Antonio de Pazos y Figueroa, Arbasia filled the walls of the brilliantly-lit enclave with frescoes of the 48 Córdoban martyrs who were slain under Moorish rule, such as Saint Eulogius, Aurea, Paul of St. Zoilus, Sisenandus, and more. Each section of the wall, divided by arch-like borders, featured three martyrs, along with an epigraph detailing their names, accomplishments, and the events surrounding their deaths. Later on, a joiner by the name of Guillermo de Orta was charged with producing the gates and tabernacle of the Sanctuary. Another builder, Hernando de Valencia, was tasked with constructing the railings.

One of the most prolific contributors to the mosque-cathedral was Antonio del Castillo. Del Castillo is credited with various paintings in the Mezquita, including the Saint Acisclus Martyrdom of Saint Pelagius, the Immaculate Virgin with Saint Philip and James, and the Denial of Saint Peter, among others, but it was the altarpiece he constructed for the Capilla de Nuestra Señora del Rosario that many consider his most impressive piece. The altarpiece, erected during the return of the wretched black plague in the 16th century, consisted of four paintings. In the center was the plump, rosy-cheeked figure of Mother Mary, carrying the toddler Jesus in her arms. The way Mary delicately caresses her child's foot is a detail appreciated by art experts, as it showcases the humanity Del Castillo infused into his paintings. To the left of this painting is one of another Córdoban martyr, Saint Sebastian, who, sporting only a loincloth, poses with an arm stretched over his head. To the right was Saint Roch, pictured with a traveling staff and his robe hiked up to show the wound on his thigh. Finally, there was a painting of a crucified Christ displayed above the Virgin and Child, set against a stormy night sky.

As suggested by the engravings of one of the arches in the southern half of the Mezquita, in 1618, Bishop Diego de Mardones oversaw the construction of yet another new main chapel and transept for the mosque-cathedral. The 50,000 ducats in donations he received were solely used for the Altar Mayor, or "main altar" of the new main chapel. Unfortunately, due to a number of setbacks, construction was only completed in 1653 under the guardianship of the Jesuit monk Alonso Matias. It was Matias who personally supervised the finishing touches of the altar, a fantastic and large work of art fabricated out of marble, bronze, and gold. The official website of the Mezquita provides a description of the elaborate setup: "The altarpiece is structured into a base, a main body formed by 3 aisles through 4 composite capital columns and a top. The tabernacle is flanked by the canvases of Saiant Acisclus and Saint Victoria, with the Allegory of the Church and the Allegory of Abundance corresponding to these at the top. The upper vault is presided over by the painting of the Assumption, flanked by the canvases of martyrs Saint Eulogius...and Saint Flora... who are crowned with the effigies of Justice and Temperance. Moreover, to the sides of the martyr figures are the sculptures of Saint Peter and Saint Paul...In the top...a relief of God the Father separated from the first body through a cornice with a pediment over which the representations of Faith and Hope rest, holding a wreath..."

Despite all the revisions, touch-ups, and additions the mosque-cathedral received, the Christian landlords of the Mezquita continued to make enhancements, spearheading at least two major projects with each new century. In the summer of 1742, Archdeacon José Diaz de Recalde announced his plans to rebuild the choir stalls, attaching to it a budget of 120,000 reales. Dozens of sculptors submitted their sketches, but the job was ultimately rewarded to Duque Cornejo.

Construction of the new choir stalls started in mid-March of 1748. The finished ensemble, which were split in two and pressed up against opposite walls facing the congregational pews, featured a total of 53 seats, with 30 of them on the upper level and the remaining 23 on the lower level. In September 1752, Cornejo went to work on the highlight of the enclave, the episcopal throne. The lofty frame of the colossal wooden throne, fitted with a trinity of velvet seats, was designed as if it was an altarpiece itself, and carefully carved into the frame were life-sized figures reenacting scenes from the Ascension of the Lord. Finally, the piece was surmounted by the winged Archangel Raphael, wielding his sacred staff of healing.

Additionally, a pair of massive sillería, or pipe organs, was installed on the upper levels of the cathedral. The stupendous instrument resembled a large glass cabinet filled with golden pipes, topped with a smaller set of pipes encased in a chamber reminiscent of an ancient Roman temple. In the years that followed, painters glazed layers of white over several of the striped arches, and inserted more baroque-style vaults and lucernarios, or chandeliers, slowly but surely stripping away the Moorish magic of the Mezquita.

Identity Crisis

"A droplet of the lifeblood

Transforms a piece of dead rock into a living

heart;

An impressive sound, into a song of solicitude,

A refrain or rapture or a melody of mirth..." - Allama Muhammad Iqbal, "The Mosque of Cordoba" (1933)

It was only in the 19th century that the Catholic Church finally hit the brakes when it came to Christianizing the Mezquita. Following a period of backlash from local authorities and members of the public alike, who chastised the Church for drowning out the most timeless and irreplaceable parts of the mosque-cathedral, the Cathedral Chapter grudgingly instituted another series of refurbishments that would undo their most conspicuous blunders. A new crew of laborers disassembled the baroque vaults, tore down several chapels, and scrubbed the white paint off the horseshoe arches, recovering the original prayer niche and the distinctive red-and-white wedges on the Arabesque arches. In the early decades of the 20th century, the hired hands reconstructed the Moorish doors on the eastern wing of the Mezquita. The majority of the current mosque-cathedral's Islamic elements are products of these restorations.

The revival of the Mezquita's Islamic roots, a campaign that still persists to this day, was devised by the Spanish liberals of the era. The Spanish Moors were to the liberals a fascinating and rebellious people who generously contributed to and fostered the evolution of the local culture. Most importantly, they were an indispensable fragment of Spanish history. Conversely, they viewed the Catholic Church and the state as authoritarians determined to snuff out anything they deemed a threat.

When the mosque-cathedral was officially named a national monument in 1882, liberals fought for and eventually secured an equal number of seats on the provincial monuments commission. From the inside, liberals were able to persuade the rest of the board members to sign off on projects that aimed to recover the Moorish spirit of the Mezquita. Ricardo Velázquez Bosco was the chief architect employed to direct the new restorations. Bosco, a protege of Eugene Viollet-le-Duc, rebuilt the roofs, as well as the doors of the Viziers and the Capilla de Villaviciosa. He then prised off the old flooring and coated the bare ground with a fresh layer of Macael marble.

In the 1930s, the Mezquita's name was in local headlines once again. Astonishingly, a number of Republicans – motivated by their political campaigns in North Africa – proposed that the Muslims be welcomed back into the Mezquita, even going so far as to suggest that the transept be torn down and recreated in Moorish fashion. For the next four decades, the monumental proposition was reviewed by board members of the World Heritage Foundation and international consultants, and the discussion even became a topic in the nation's most prestigious architectural magazine, *Arquitectura*. To the dismay of the campaigners, the International Council on Monuments and Sites (ICOMOS) rejected their proposal to tear down the crucero in 1973, a conference that transpired on the grounds of the Mezquita itself. ICOMOS officials cited the

1964 Venice Charter and declared that the transept be left intact, for it was proof of "religious and cultural coexistence," a term known as "convivencia."

The issue of whether the landlords of the Mezquita were actually playing by the rules of convivencia was another story. As the decades rolled on by, Spanish Muslims became more and more aggravated by their incapacity to pray in an establishment they considered rightfully theirs. This resentment was only exacerbated by the Church's flaunting of authority, and what many called an attempt to "whitewash" the history of the mosque-cathedral.

Muslim protests were sparked by the publication of a Church-authored brochure in 1981. The brochure began with a promising start, hailing the mosque-cathedral as the "foremost monument o the Islamic West," but the rest of the brochure was written in what many saw as a grossly distorted interpretation of the Mezquita's history. According to the brochure, "Since then and without missing a single day in this beautiful and grandiose temple, the Cathedral Chapter has celebrated solemn worship, and the Christian community comes together to listen to the Word of God and to participate in the Sacraments." The brochure then proceeded to minimize the Islamic history of the Mezquita by referring to this period as the "Muslim Intervention," and the brochure further angered its Muslim and liberal readers by reminding them to "be respectful with the identity of this Christian temple."

The ongoing tensions between the local Muslims and Christians inevitably trickled into the 21st century. In 2006, Muslims were outraged to learn that the Church, which operated the mosque-cathedral's official website, had quietly removed the word "mosque" from that site and other online publications. There now exists two nearly identical websites that claim to host the official website of the mosque-cathedral, one registered under the Mezquita and the other under the Cathedral Chapter of Córdoba. Still, the Church seemed undaunted; three years later, Bishop Demetrio Fernandez caused more uproar when he registered the mosque-cathedral under his own name, a controversial act that set him back only €30.

On April 1, 2010, the festering tensions finally bubbled over, resulting in the first major physical confrontation between the sides. Six Muslim visitors, who came with a tour group of 100 other visitors from Austria, silently knelt down under a cluster of striped arches and began to pray. Security guards approached them almost at once, ordering the men to rise to their feet. The following statement released by the bishop's office described what ensued following their refusal: "They replied by attacking the security guards, 2 of whom suffered serious injuries." Over a dozen police officers were dispatched to the scene to break up the scuffle, only to be allegedly attacked by the tourists. In the end, two of the six were apprehended, and a knife was supposedly confiscated from one of the arrested. The bishop's office concluded, "They provoked in a pre-planned fashion what was a deplorable episode of violence."

Naturally, the event caught the attention of the Muslim and liberal communities. Mansur Escudero of Junta Islamica was among those who pointed out the hypocrisy of the Church, complaining, "[The Catholic Church argues] that canon law does not allow Muslims to pray there, [but] they have been happy to permit visiting Saudi princes and other dignitaries, including Saddam Hussein, to pray."

In 2014, an international petition, which garnered close to 100,000 signatures, was submitted to UNESCO and the Andalusian authorities via the Change.org platform. In it, petitioners were campaigning for authority of the historic monument (and World Heritage Site as of 1984) to be transferred to public ownership. After much deliberation, UNESCO proposed a plan that they hoped would appease all parties involved - it was decided that the monument, though classified as a cathedral, would continue to hold the title of "Mezquita."

In 2016, the newly-elected mayor, Isabel Ambrosio, of the Spanish Socialist Workers' Party, pledged in her inaugural speech to "return [the] title [of the Mezquita] to the public domain." That said, while the Catholic Church has accepted this appellation, they have yet to renounce ownership of the mosque-cathedral complex. For the time being, one can only hope that the Muslims of Christians of Córdoba eventually bridge the gaps and are able to celebrate the Mezquita together.

Online Resources

Other books about Spanish history by Charles River Editors

Other books about Great Mosque of Cordoba on Amazon

Bibliography

Ruggles, D F. *The Stratigraphy of Forgetting: The Great Mosque of Cordoba and Its Contested Legacy*. 2011, www.masjed.ir/Content/media/article/9781441973047-c1 (1)_0.pdf. Accessed 30 May 2018.

Editors, P. H. (2017, February 8). THE GREAT MOSQUE OF CÓRDOBA. Retrieved May 30, 2018, from https://pufflesandhoneyadventures.wordpress.com/2017/02/08/the-great-mosque-of-cordoba/

Editors, U. (2013). History of Cordoba. Retrieved May 30, 2018, from http://www.uco.es/pci-uco-kenitra/cordoba.htm

Editors, O. R. (2017, June 14). The Great Mosque of Cordoba, a timeless masterpiece. Retrieved May 30, 2018, from https://omrania.com/inspiration/great-mosque-cordoba-timeless-masterpiece/

Hildebrand, T. (2012). Architectural Origins of the Mosque of Cordoba. Retrieved May 30, 2018, from https://digitalcommons.unl.edu/cgi/viewcontent.cgi?article=1174&context=nebanthro

Editors, W. A. (2017). Mosque of Cordoba. Retrieved May 30, 2018, from https://en.wikiarquitectura.com/building/mosque-of-cordoba/

El-Shorbagy, A. (2012). The Great Mosque of Cordoba (784-786): A Controversial Architectural Statement in the History of Both Christians and Muslims. Retrieved May 30, 2018, from https://architecture.knoji.com/the-great-mosque-of-cordoba-784786-a-controversial-architectural-statement-in-the-history-of-both-christians-and-muslims/

Llorente, M. S. (2018). Great Mosque of Córdoba. Retrieved May 30, 2018, from http://www.discoverislamicart.org/database_item.php?id=monument;isl;es;mon01;1;en

Dodds, J. (2012). The Great Mosque of Cordoba. Retrieved May 30, 2018, from http://www.learn.columbia.edu/ma/htm/dj_islam/ma_dji_discuss_cordoba.htm

Saoud, R. (2015). The Mosque of Cordoba. Retrieved May 30, 2018, from http://www.muslimheritage.com/article/mosque-cordoba

Calderwood, E. (2015, April 10). The Reconquista of the Mosque of Córdoba. Retrieved May 30, 2018, from http://foreignpolicy.com/2015/04/10/the-reconquista-of-the-mosque-of-cordoba-spain-catholic-church-islam/

Editors, L. P. (2017). Mezquita. Retrieved May 30, 2018, from https://www.lonelyplanet.com/spain/cordoba/attractions/mezquita/a/poi-sig/1189075/360732

Editors, J. F. (2016). Interesting facts about the Mosque–Cathedral of Córdoba. Retrieved May 30, 2018, from http://justfunfacts.com/interesting-facts-about-the-mosque-cathedral-of-cordoba/

Mirmobiny, S. (2014). The Great Mosque of Cordoba. Retrieved May 30, 2018, from https://www.khanacademy.org/humanities/ap-art-history/early-europe-and-colonial-americas/ap-art-islamic-world-medieval/a/the-great-mosque-of-cordoba

Editors, T. H. (2014, December 23). The Great Mosque of Cordoba. Retrieved May 30, 2018, from http://www.travelingthruhistory.com/the-great-mosque-of-cordoba-3/

Editors, A. V. (2015). Mezquita Cordoba. Retrieved May 30, 2018, from http://www.absolutevisit.com/travel/Mezquita-Cordoba/facts-and-history

Editors, N. F. (2015, April 25). The Great Mosque of Córdoba, the majestic Mezquita. Retrieved May 30, 2018, from https://notesfromcamelidcountry.net/2015/04/25/the-great-mosque-of-cordoba-the-majestic-mezquita/

Nayler, M. (2017, June 11). A Brief History of the Mosque-Cathedral of Córdoba. Retrieved May 30, 2018, from https://theculturetrip.com/europe/spain/articles/the-history-of-the-mosque-cathedral-of-cordoba-in-1-minute-2/

Editors, N. P. (2017, February 11). CORDOBA AND ONCE UPON A TIME. Retrieved May 30, 2018, from https://noparticularplacetogo.net/tag/the-mosque-cathedral-of-cordoba/

Editors, M. C. (2018). The history. Retrieved May 30, 2018, from https://mezquita-catedraldecordoba.es/en/descubre-el-monumento/la-historia/

Lamprakos, M. (2016, December 12). Memento Mauri: The Mosque-Cathedral of Cordoba. Retrieved May 30, 2018, from http://we-aggregate.org/piece/memento-mauri-the-mosque-cathedral-of-cordoba

Nowell, C. (2017). Mosque-Cathedral. Retrieved May 30, 2018, from https://www.atlasobscura.com/places/mosquecathedral

Khoury, N. N. (1996). The Meaning of the Great Mosque of Cordoba in the Tenth Century. Retrieved May 30, 2018, from https://faculty.risd.edu/bcampbel/Khoury_The Meaning of the Great Mosque of Cordoba[1].pdf

Del Posadero, P. (2016, May 16). 5 legends of Córdoba that will make you come back to visit it. Retrieved May 30, 2018, from https://www.patiodelposadero.com/en/five-legends-of-cordoba-that-will-make-you-come-back-to-visit-it/

Editors, C. M. (2017). Reimaging the Cordoba Mosque. Retrieved May 30, 2018, from https://www.criticalmuslim.io/reimaging-the-cordoba-mosque/

Editors, F. H. (2016). Traveling to The Great Mosque of Cordoba Spain. Retrieved May 30, 2018, from https://www.familyholiday.net/the-great-mosque-of-cordoba-spain/

Gedal, N. (2011, December 14). The Great Mosque of Cordoba: Geometric Analysis. Retrieved May 30, 2018, from http://islamic-arts.org/2011/the-great-mosque-of-cordoba-geometric-analysis/

Witcombe, C. L. (2017). MOSQUE AT CÓRDOBA, SPAIN. Retrieved May 30, 2018, from http://witcombe.sbc.edu/sacredplaces/cordoba.html

Editors, M. C. (2015). The History of Cordoba. Retrieved May 30, 2018, from http://www.mezquitadecordoba.org/en/roman-period.asp

Editors, A. C. (2017). The Roman Cordoba: Presentation. Retrieved May 31, 2018, from http://www.artencordoba.com/en/roman-cordoba/roman-cordoba.html

Lendering, J. (2018, April 4). Corduba (Córdoba). Retrieved May 31, 2018, from http://www.livius.org/articles/place/corduba-cordoba/

Editors, S. F. (2013, August 30). Roman Spain. Retrieved May 31, 2018, from https://www.spanish-fiestas.com/history/romans/

De Trolio III, P. (2015). THE STRANGE STORY OF CORDOBA'S DISPUTED CATHEDRAL. Retrieved May 31, 2018, from http://reginamag.com/the-strange-story-of-cordobas-disputed-cathedral/

Editors, E. B. (2018, February 14). Janus. Retrieved May 31, 2018, from https://www.britannica.com/topic/Janus-Roman-god

Davenport, C. (2018, January 1). How Janus, the Roman god of beginnings and endings, would celebrate 2018. Retrieved May 31, 2018, from http://www.abc.net.au/news/2018-01-01/new-year-janus-the-roman-god-of-beginnings-and-endings/9296694

Gill, N. S. (2017, June 8). Who Was the Ancient Roman God Janus? Retrieved May 31, 2018, from https://www.thoughtco.com/ancient-roman-god-janus-112605

Editors, R. A. (2013). Sacrifices in Roman religion. Retrieved May 31, 2018, from http://www.romanarmy.net/sacrifices.shtml

Editors, M. C. (2016). Visigoth Period. Retrieved May 31, 2018, from http://www.mezquitadecordoba.org/en/visigoth-period.asp

Editors, M. C. (2018). Visigoth Basilica of San Vicente. Retrieved May 31, 2018, from https://mezquita-catedraldecordoba.es/en/descubre-el-monumento/el-edificio/basilica-visigoda-de-san-vicente/

Editors, S. N. (2010). Visigoths in Spain. Retrieved May 31, 2018, from http://www.spainthenandnow.com/spanish-history/visigoths-in-spain

Editors, S. N. (2016). The Great Mosque of Córdoba. La Mezquita. Retrieved May 31, 2018, from http://www.spainthenandnow.com/spanish-architecture/the-great-mosque-of-cordoba-la-mezquita

Editors, C. O. (2018). St. Vincent Saragossa. Retrieved May 31, 2018, from https://www.catholic.org/saints/saint.php?saint_id=724

Editors, V. C. (2018). St. Vincent of Saragossa, Deacon, first Martyr of Spain. Retrieved May 31, 2018, from http://www.stvincentscathedral.org/page/st_vincent_of_saragossa_deacon_first_martyr_of_spain

Editors, H. C. (2015). Old town of Cordoba. Retrieved May 31, 2018, from http://www.heritagecultureblog.eu/cordoba.php

Nitol, F. (2016, April 25). Once Upon a Time Europe Had Its Very Own Flourishing Islamic City. Retrieved May 31, 2018, from http://mvslim.com/jewels-muslim-world-cordoba/

Editors, E. C. (2004). Abd Ar-Rahman I. Retrieved May 31, 2018, from https://www.encyclopedia.com/people/history/spanish-and-portuguese-history-biographies/abd-ar-rahman-i

Editors, T. B. (2018). Biography of Emir de al-Andalus Abd ar-Rahman o Abderramán I (731-788). Retrieved May 31, 2018, from http://thebiography.us/en/abd-ar-Rahman-i

Editors, A. A. (2015, November 25). Abd Ar-Rahman I - The Architect Of Moorish Spain. Retrieved May 31, 2018, from http://www.arabamerica.com/abd-ar-Rahman-architect-moorish-spain/

O'Doherty, E. (2013, May 29). The Europeans, no 22: Abd ar-Rahman I. Retrieved May 31, 2018, from https://www.irishtimes.com/culture/the-europeans-no-22-abd-ar-Rahman-i-1.1408902

Editors, M. C. (2018). Expansion of Abd ar-Rahman II. Retrieved May 31, 2018, from https://mezquita-catedraldecordoba.es/en/descubre-el-monumento/el-edificio/ampliacion-de-abderraman-ii/

Editors, M. C. (2018). Intervention of Abd ar-Rahman III. Retrieved May 31, 2018, from https://mezquita-catedraldecordoba.es/en/descubre-el-monumento/el-edificio/intervencion-de-abderraman-iii/

Editors, Y. A. (2012, November). The Colors of Córdoba, Spain. Retrieved May 31, 2018, from https://youngadventuress.com/2012/11/colors-of-cordoba.html

Editors, H. M. (2016). QUOTES REGARDING MUSLIMS IN SPAIN:. Retrieved May 31, 2018, from http://www.hispanicmuslims.com/andalusia/quotes.html

Editors, C. 2. (2017). Mezquita Mosque and Cathedral. Retrieved May 31, 2018, from https://www.cordoba24.info/english/html/mezquita.html

Editors, S. F. (2015, July 6). Mezquita – Great Mosque of Cordoba. Retrieved May 31, 2018, from https://www.spanish-fiestas.com/attractions/mezquita/

Burgen, S. (2016, March 13). Córdoba rejects Catholic church's claim to own mosque-cathedral. Retrieved May 31, 2018, from https://www.theguardian.com/world/2016/mar/13/cordoba-catholic-churchs-claim-mosque-cathedral

Editors, H. H. (2011, October 4). The 'Abbasid Revolution. Retrieved May 31, 2018, from http://www.historyinanhour.com/2011/10/04/the-'abbasid-revolution/

Editors, A. M. (2012, October 23). THE GREAT MOSQUE OF CORDOBA. Retrieved May 31, 2018, from http://architecturalmoleskine.blogspot.com/2012/10/the-great-mosque-of-cordoba.html

Editors, E. B. (2016, June 20). Minaret. Retrieved June 1, 2018, from https://www.britannica.com/art/minaret-architecture

Editors, M. C. (2017). The first expansion (821-852). Retrieved June 1, 2018, from http://www.mezquitadecordoba.org/en/history-expansion-mosque.asp

Murphy, J. C. (2012, March 31). The Mosque of Cordova. Retrieved June 1, 2018, from http://islamic-arts.org/2012/mosque-of-cordova/

Editors, I. M. (2009). Mosque: Definition and parts. Retrieved June 1, 2018, from http://museoimaginadodecordoba.es/2009/mezquita-definicion-y-sus-partes?lang=en

Editors, A. Z. (2013, August 1). The Mosque of Córdoba ~ A Glimpse into Moorish Spain. Retrieved June 1, 2018, from http://arabiczeal.com/mosque-crdoba-glimpse-moorish-spain/

Editors, T. C. (2014). The Mosque of Abderraman I. Retrieved June 1, 2018, from https://english.turismodecordoba.org/seccion/the-mosque-of-abderraman-i

Editors, A. C. (2017). Door of Saint Stephen. Retrieved June 1, 2018, from http://www.artencordoba.com/en/mosque-cordoba/door-san-esteban.html

Editors, A. C. (2017). First Extension by Abd Ar-Rahman II. Retrieved June 1, 2018, from http://www.artencordoba.com/en/mosque-cordoba/first-extension-abd-ar-Rahman-II.html

Editors, B. C. (2017). Ibn 'Idari on the Mosque of Córdoba. Retrieved June 1, 2018, from http://bridgingcultures.neh.gov/muslimjourneys/items/show/293

Editors, H. M. (2016, July 21). Iberia – part 6: Fall of the Caliphate of Córdoba. Retrieved June 1, 2018, from http://historandmor.blogspot.com/2016/07/iberia-part-6-fall-of-caliphate-of.html

Editors, A. (2015). THE MOSQUE CATHEDRAL. Retrieved June 1, 2018, from http://www.andalucia.com/cities/cordoba/mosque.htm

Editors, R. (2018, February 10). Al-Hakam II. Retrieved June 1, 2018, from https://www.revolvy.com/topic/Al-Hakam II

Editors, U. A. (2013, February 5). Maqsura de la mezquita de Córdoba. Retrieved June 1, 2018, from http://unratodearte.blogspot.com/2013/02/maqsura-de-la-mezquita-de-cordoba.html

Editors, A. N. (2011). Mezquita de Córdoba. Retrieved June 1, 2018, from https://archnet.org/sites/2715/media_contents/2222

Editors, N. A. (2018). Eight Pointed Star Rug Design. Retrieved June 1, 2018, from https://nazmiyalantiquerugs.com/resources/guide/motifs-symbols/eight-pointed-stars-rug-design-motif/

Nicanor, P. (2009). Geometry in Islamic Architecture. Retrieved June 1, 2018, from http://psdg.pbworks.com/w/page/19548743/Geometry in Islamic Architecture

Iqbal, A. M. (2012, March 16). The Mosque Of Cordoba. Retrieved June 1, 2018, from https://www.poemhunter.com/poem/the-mosque-of-cordoba/

Editors, I. A. (2011, March 19). The Mosque of Cordoba: La Mezquita. Retrieved June 4, 2018, from http://islamic-arts.org/2011/the-mosque-of-cardoba-la-mezquita/

Editors, B. C. (2009, September 4). Muslim Spain (711-1492). Retrieved June 4, 2018, from http://www.bbc.co.uk/religion/religions/islam/history/spain_1.shtml

Editors, A. C. (2017). Orange Trees Courtyard. Retrieved June 4, 2018, from http://www.artencordoba.com/en/mosque-cordoba/orange-tree-courtyard.html

Editors, M. C. (2017). History of the Courtyard of the Orange Trees. Retrieved June 4, 2018, from http://www.mezquitadecordoba.org/en/history-courtyard-orange-trees.asp

Editors, S. C. (2015). Patio de los Naranjos (Orange Tree Courtyard) in Cordoba Cathedral-Mosque. Retrieved June 4, 2018, from http://www.spainisculture.com/en/jardines_historicos/cordoba/patio_de_los_naranjos_de_la_iglesia_catedral_de_cordoba.html

Editors, A. (2017). The Route of the Caliphate. Retrieved June 4, 2018, from http://www.andalucia.org/en/routes/the-route-of-the-caliphate/

Editors, M. C. (2017). The Caliphate Route and the Mosque of Cordoba. Retrieved June 4, 2018, from http://www.mezquitadecordoba.org/en/route-caliphate.asp

Editors, S. C. (2017). Route of the Caliphate. Retrieved June 4, 2018, from http://www.spainisculture.com/en/rutas_culturales/ruta_del_califato.html

Editors, S. D. (2007, April 4). Mezquita de Cordoba. Retrieved June 4, 2018, from http://www.sacred-destinations.com/spain/cordoba-mezquita

Bartetzko, D. (2014, March 24). Is Cordoba denying its Islamic heritage? Retrieved June 4, 2018, from https://en.qantara.de/content/la-mezquita-in-cordoba-is-cordoba-denying-its-islamic-heritage

Editors, S. N. (2009). Cordoba Mosque: Calligraphy and Imagery. Retrieved June 4, 2018, from http://www.spainthenandnow.com/spanish-architecture/cordoba-mosque-calligraphy-and-imagery

García, C. H. (2017). Biography of Hisham II (965-1013). Retrieved June 4, 2018, from http://thebiography.us/en/hisham-ii

Editors, M. C. (2017). The Mosque-Cathedral of Cordoba. Retrieved June 4, 2018, from https://mezquita-catedraldecordoba.es/site/assets/files/1060/folleto_ingles_web.pdf

Editors, Q. C. (2015, April 2). What Was Europe Like Under Moorish Rule? Retrieved June 4, 2018, from http://www.slate.com/blogs/quora/2015/04/02/what_was_europe_like_under_the_rule_of_the_moors.html

Editors, N. (2011, May 30). Saint Ferdinand III of Castile. Retrieved June 4, 2018, from http://www.nobility.org/2011/05/30/may-30/

Editors, M. C. (2017). History of the Tower of the Mosque of Cordoba. Retrieved June 4, 2018, from http://www.mezquitadecordoba.org/en/history-tower-mosque.asp

Editors, M. C. (2017). Bell Tower. Retrieved June 4, 2018, from https://mezquita-catedraldecordoba.es/en/descubre-el-monumento/el-edificio/torre-campanario/

Cohen, M. (2016). Statue of St Ferdinand III of Castile. Retrieved June 4, 2018, from http://manuelcohen.photoshelter.com/image/I00007MtXSI5BndQ

Mahmoud, N. (2014, June 9). BLOG: Before converting Hagia Sophia, look at the mosque-cathedral of Cordoba. Retrieved June 4, 2018, from http://www.hurriyetdailynews.com/blog-before-converting-hagia-sophia-look-at-the-mosque-cathedral-of-cordoba-67578

Editors, A. C. (2017). Royal Chapel. Retrieved June 4, 2018, from http://www.artencordoba.com/en/mosque-cordoba/royal-chapel-cathedral.html

Editors, A. S. (2017). The Mesquita in Cordoba. Retrieved June 4, 2018, from https://www.atroshenko.com/travelphotos/NSTravCordobaA.html

Editors, H. S. (2017). Cordoba Cathedral - The Mezquita - Tourist Attractions Cordoba. Retrieved June 4, 2018, from http://www.hotels-spain-accommodation.com/andalucia/cordoba/mezquita/

Malik, K. (2015, May 11). A cathedral, a mosque, a clash of civilizations. Retrieved June 4, 2018, from https://kenanmalik.wordpress.com/2015/05/11/a-cathedral-a-mosque-a-clash-of-civilizations/

Editors, M. C. (2017). Villaviciosa Chapel. Retrieved June 4, 2018, from https://mezquita-catedraldecordoba.es/en/descubre-el-monumento/el-edificio/capilla-de-villaviciosa/

Editors, A. C. (2017). Primitive Main Chapel. Retrieved June 4, 2018, from http://www.artencordoba.com/en/mosque-cordoba/old-main-chapel-cathedral.html

Editors, M. C. (2017). Chapel of the Conversion of Saint Paul. Retrieved June 4, 2018, from https://mezquita-catedraldecordoba.es/en/descubre-el-monumento/capillas/capilla-de-la-conversion-de-san-pablo/

Editors, M. C. (2017). Chapel of San Esteban and San Bartolomé. Retrieved June 4, 2018, from https://mezquita-catedraldecordoba.es/en/descubre-el-monumento/capillas/capilla-de-san-esteban-y-san-bartolome/

Editors, M. C. (2017). Chapel of the Nativity of Our Lady. Retrieved June 4, 2018, from https://mezquita-catedraldecordoba.es/en/descubre-el-monumento/capillas/capilla-de-la-natividad-de-nuestra-senora/

Editors, M. C. (2017). Chapel of the Souls of Purgatory. Retrieved June 4, 2018, from https://mezquita-catedraldecordoba.es/en/descubre-el-monumento/capillas/capilla-de-las-animas-del-purgatorio/

Editors, M. C. (2017). Chapel of Our Lady of Conception. Retrieved June 4, 2018, from https://mezquita-catedraldecordoba.es/en/descubre-el-monumento/capillas/capilla-de-nuestra-senora-de-la-concepcion/

Editors, M. C. (2017). Chapel of Santa Teresa. Retrieved June 4, 2018, from https://mezquita-catedraldecordoba.es/en/descubre-el-monumento/capillas/capilla-de-santa-teresa/

Editors, M. C. (2017). Chapel of Santa Inés. Retrieved June 4, 2018, from https://mezquita-catedraldecordoba.es/en/descubre-el-monumento/capillas/capilla-de-santa-ines/

Editors, A. C. (2017). Altar Mayor. Retrieved June 4, 2018, from http://www.artencordoba.com/en/mosque-cordoba/main-altar-cathedral.html

Editors, M. C. (2017). Main Altarpiece. Retrieved June 4, 2018, from https://mezquita-catedraldecordoba.es/en/descubre-el-monumento/obras-maestras/retablo-mayor/

Editors, H. C. (2014, January 4). Reconquest of Spain. Retrieved June 4, 2018, from https://www.history.com/this-day-in-history/reconquest-of-spain

Editors, W. F. (2015). Ceilings in Córdoba. Retrieved June 4, 2018, from http://wtfarthistory.com/post/24471011647/ceilings-in-córdoba

Editors, M. C. (2017). Processional custody of Corpus Christi. Retrieved June 4, 2018, from https://mezquita-catedraldecordoba.es/en/descubre-el-monumento/obras-maestras/custodia-procesional-del-corpus-christi/

Editors, M. C. (2017). Capilla Mayor, Crucero y Coro. Retrieved June 4, 2018, from https://mezquita-catedraldecordoba.es/descubre-el-monumento/el-edificio/capilla-mayor-crucero-y-coro/

Editors, A. C. (2017). Belfry Tower. Retrieved June 4, 2018, from http://www.artencordoba.com/en/mosque-cordoba/belfry-tower.html

Editors, M. C. (2017). The Holy Supper. Retrieved June 4, 2018, from https://mezquita-catedraldecordoba.es/en/descubre-el-monumento/obras-maestras/la-santa-cena/

Editors, C. C. (2017). Parroquia del Sagrario. Retrieved June 4, 2018, from https://cabildocatedraldecordoba.es/en/parroquia-del-sagrario/

Editors, M. C. (2017). Altarpiece of Our Lady of the Rosary. Retrieved June 4, 2018, from https://mezquita-catedraldecordoba.es/en/descubre-el-monumento/obras-maestras/retablo-de-nuestra-senora-del-rosario/

Editors, M. C. (2017). Choir stalls. Retrieved June 4, 2018, from https://mezquita-catedraldecordoba.es/en/descubre-el-monumento/obras-maestras/silleria-de-coro/

Hopler, W. (2017, July 15). Meet Archangel Raphael, the Angel of Healing. Retrieved June 4, 2018, from https://www.thoughtco.com/meet-archangel-raphael-angel-of-healing-124716

Editors, G. P. (2015, April 30). What Mosque? White-washing Islamic History in Spain. Retrieved June 4, 2018, from http://georgiapoliticalreview.com/what-mosque-white-ashing-islamic-history-in-spain/

Kassam, A. (2014, December 5). Córdoba's Mosque-Cathedral in name-change row. Retrieved June 4, 2018, from https://www.theguardian.com/world/2014/dec/05/cordoba-mosque-cathedral-name-change-row-andalusia

Tremlett, G. (2010, April 1). Two arrested after fight in Cordoba's former mosque. Retrieved June 4, 2018, from https://www.theguardian.com/world/2010/apr/01/muslim-catholic-mosque-fight

Knapp, R. C. (1983). *Roman Córdoba*. University of California Press.

Darke, D. (2006). *Syria*. Bradt Travel Guides.

Ruggles, D. F. (2011). *Islamic Gardens and Landscapes*. University of Pennsylvania Press.

Free Books by Charles River Editors

We have brand new titles available for free most days of the week. To see which of our titles are currently free, click on this link.

Discounted Books by Charles River Editors

We have titles at a discount price of just 99 cents everyday. To see which of our titles are currently 99 cents, [click on this link](#).

Printed in Great Britain
by Amazon